IMPLEMENTING EFFECTIVE CODE REVIEWS

HOW TO BUILD AND MAINTAIN CLEAN CODE

Giuliana Carullo

Apress®

Implementing Effective Code Reviews: How to Build and Maintain Clean Code

Giuliana Carullo
Dublin, Ireland

ISBN-13 (pbk): 978-1-4842-6161-3 ISBN-13 (electronic): 978-1-4842-6162-0
https://doi.org/10.1007/978-1-4842-6162-0

Managing Director, Apress Media LLC: Welmoed Spahr
Acquisitions Editor: Shiva Ramachandran
Development Editor: Rita Fernando
Coordinating Editor: Rita Fernando

Cover designed by eStudioCalamar

Distributed to the book trade worldwide by Springer Science+Business Media New York, 1 New York Plaza, New York, NY 100043. Phone 1-800-SPRINGER, fax (201) 348-4505, e-mail orders-ny@springer-sbm.com, or visit www.springeronline.com. Apress Media, LLC is a California LLC and the sole member (owner) is Springer Science + Business Media Finance Inc (SSBM Finance Inc). SSBM Finance Inc is a **Delaware** corporation.

For information on translations, please e-mail booktranslations@springernature.com; for reprint, paperback, or audio rights, please e-mail bookpermissions@springernature.com.

Apress titles may be purchased in bulk for academic, corporate, or promotional use. eBook versions and licenses are also available for most titles. For more information, reference our Print and eBook Bulk Sales web page at http://www.apress.com/bulk-sales.

Any source code or other supplementary material referenced by the author in this book is available to readers on GitHub via the book's product page, located at www.apress.com/9781484261613. For more detailed information, please visit http://www.apress.com/source-code.

Printed on acid-free paper

To Simone, Sofia, and Matteo (Mone, Fofi, and Petteio), who added plenty of joy to my life.

Contents

Contents

About the Author

Giuliana Carullo, CCSK, PSM certified, is a Research Engineering Manager at Tenable. With over 15 years of engineering experience, she has grown her expertise mainly in the networking, security, cloud computing, telecommunications, and Internet of Things (IoT) industries. Through her career, she has worn many hats, including researcher, engineer, project manager, and engineering manager. Giuliana has been doing research in a number of application fields for over 7 years, 5 of which were devoted to the InfoSec area. She dealt with research in a number of application fields, from academia to industrial research, within SMEs (small and mid-size enterprises) and corporations, including Intel and Ericsson. As the author of 15 research papers and several books, Giuliana loves to make even difficult concepts entertaining and easy to grasp.

About the Technical Reviewer

Alex Kondov is a software engineer who has worked for both early-stage startups and large media giants such as the *Financial Times*. Throughout his career, he's faced both the challenges of visually rich applications and the problems of distribution in microservices architectures. This has helped him find the balance between technology and business and see the benefits of clean code no matter the product.

Preface

I confess that I have been blind as a mole, but it is better to learn wisdom late than never to learn it at all.

—Sherlock Holmes in Arthur Conan Doyle's "The Man with the Twisted Lip" (1891)

When I was 8 years old, I decided that I wanted to be a computer scientist. Since then, all my career and the majority of my interests have been oriented toward technology, programming, and getting better at it. I spent the majority of my life developing my software engineering skills and learning tips and tricks on how to write beautiful code. Over 15 years, I've had time and pleasure to learn and set in place coding standards and good coding practices.

The more I learned, the more I realized that a software engineer is not just one who writes code. Being an engineer isn't just about coding or looking up how to solve a bug. That's just 20% of our job. Coding is not just coding. After reading a lot of the most valuable existing books from programming languages, good practices, concurrency to security, I couldn't really find a comprehensive view on the topic.

Hence, this book was born. It addresses some of the major trade-offs a lot of companies and software engineers out there need to consistently make:

1. What does good software look like?

2. Do I really need good coding practices? To what extent?

3. What if I need to keep going with the development process and have little time to check the code for standards and quality?

4. Which kinds of processes do I really need?

5. How do I perform a code review?

6. What to avoid during code reviews?

7. Is it only about scanning code?

Who This Book Is For

If you're like me and you think that coding is an art, not just following the syntax of the programming language of your choice, this book is right for you. If you are the "get it out there quick" person, keep on reading; this book was designed with you in mind.

This book is aimed at people with at least some experience with programming in some sort of language: C, C++, Java, or Python. It could be easier for object-oriented programming folks to go through the book, but a lot of concepts discussed in the book are general enough to be the foundation of good coding.

Snippets of code are in Python: it is a so versatile and powerful language that it allows for mighty smells. Love it!

Some more advanced chapters—like concurrency and security—might require some more focus to make them your own if you are fairly new to them. But, no worries, keep going; it will be rewarding and it will give you the right tools to be at the top of your game.

This book is for

- Passionate programmers willing to go the extra mile and be better at their jobs. It will help you lead a happier and easier life. It might even help you earn a raise.

- People who just started to program. This book will power up your programming skills. By learning good habits from the start, you will avoid wasting time on common errors.

- Software engineers of all kinds. Knowing a programming language is not enough to be good at it. You need to use foundational concepts, clean coding, and team work skills to use your programming skills wisely.

- More experienced IT people in search for a quick guide on how to review code.

We are not here to talk about theoretical mumbo jumbo. We are going to talk about practical guidance. And it is our duty—as professionals—to code in the best possible way, is it not?

You might think, *"Will my extra effort mean something?"* And I'd say, *"Yes! Yes, it will!"*

Six reasons why this book might not be right for you:

1. If you are looking for an entire encyclopedia on data structures, software architectures, and any possible software engineering facets, this book is not for you. Certain concepts are in pills: the book provides just the core information that can assist you in doing better choices.

2. This book is not made to impress you, *it is made to help you out*. To be handy and on point.

3. It is not a Python programming book. Not a programming book per se either. It is meant to help in *writing better code* by looking at it from several angles.

4. This book *is not boring*. If you are looking for endless mechanical chapters, wrong choice. Let's add some fun; life is too short.

5. If you are looking for specific tools on how to perform code reviews, sorry, not at this point in time. This book is meant to help you learn how to fish rather than giving you fish or pointing out at who can fish for you.

6. If your heart as a programmer is too sensible on how bad code can be, please stop. I care about you, seriously. Or, at least, read with caution, don't stress too much: there are other wonderful things in the world!

And if you get upset identifying bad things that you did, no worries, every single programmer on earth has been there!

But at the end of the day, I hope you'll enjoy it!

Introduction

"Data! Data! Data!" he cried impatiently. "I can't make bricks without clay."

—Sherlock Holmes in Arthur Conan Doyle's "The Adventure of the Copper Beeches" (1892)

This book addresses the importance of good coding practices as well as it takes a deep dive on code reviews. It is a comprehensive guide across all the main aspects to look at during code reviews. The aim is to provide practical information and examples to consider when performing them.

Much like the fictional Sherlock Holmes, we must have knowledge to make the right deductions and take the correct actions. Knowledge is data, knowing all the possible things. Wisdom is discerning between the good and the bad (potentially the ugly) and picking the right things to do.

Figure 1 shows the programming pyramid.

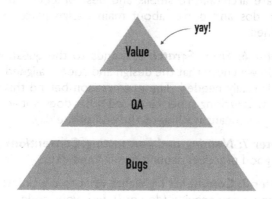

Figure 1. Programming pyramid

Bugs are the ugly and sit at the very bottom of the programming pyramid. You need to get rid of them, at all the costs. Unfortunately, oftentimes, our only concern is to just fix what is really needed and never touch again that code.

"But it was working on my laptop," they said.

In order to provide real **value**, code's **quality** needs to be assured. Sure enough, value is not only given by quality code. The fanciest code that does not achieve business goals or that does not solve people's problems would be a nice craft but would not add much value. But I believe that quality is an expression of value, as we will see later in this book.

Hence, the book focuses on code reviews from different facets in order to help achieve quality code. It is broken down into 11 chapters and it is structured as follows:

- **Chapter 1: The Art of Programming** provides a solid overview on the code review process and why it matters.

- **Chapter 2: Code Structure** deals with general structural smells to look at during code reviews including design, reusability, control structures, and APIs.

- **Chapter 3: Data Structures** takes a glance over main data structures and provides some rules of thumb to consider when designing and/or reviewing your projects.

- **Chapter 4: Design Smells** walks through main design smells to look at during a holistic review of your code.

- **Chapter 5: Software Architectures** digs deeper into software architecture smells and best practices. In particular, dos and don'ts about main design patterns are explained.

- **Chapter 6: From Scratch** responds to the question of how do we check that the design and code is aligned with what is really needed. The main reason behind this section is that writing super fancy code that does not achieve objectives means nothing at the end of the day.

- **Chapter 7: Naming and Formatting Conventions** provides good practices around naming and data.

- **Chapter 8: Comments** highlights what to check into the comments you provide (do you?) with your code.

- **Chapter 9: Concurrency, Parallelism, and Performances** provides some foundation knowledge about concurrent and parallel programming. It also introduces metrics used in this context in order to evaluate performances.

- **Chapter 10: Security** provides guidance for embedding security checks into the review process. It glances at main security principles and how to perform reviews during the development lifecycle.

- **Chapter 11: Code Reviews** closes the book by providing metrics and final remarks on code reviews. This chapter reviews how to approach code reviews depending on your role (i.e., developer, reviewer, manager).

Each chapter is addressed with a *divide-and-conquer* approach: each of them deals with issues within the topic. Thus, each chapter will walk through different practices, reasoning why they are good or bad, as well as providing some clarifying examples. Finally, a checklist ends all of them to help you during the review process of your projects.

Feedback and Errata

Feedback from readers is always more than welcome and highly valued. Let me know what you think about this book, what you liked, what you disliked, and what you would like to read in a future version on the topic.

Even if care is taken to ensure accuracy of this book, some errors can happen. As Murphy's law states:

> Anything that can go wrong will go wrong.

If you find a mistake, a typo, something missing, please report it, so I can improve the book.

More generally, you can get in touch with me by following my LinkedIn profile: www.linkedin.com/in/giucar.

Disclaimer

All opinions and concepts are my own and by no means represent the position of any of my employers past or present.

The Art of Programming

No man burdens his mind with small matters unless he has some very good reason for doing so.

—Sherlock Holmes in Sir Arthur Conan Doyle's
"A Study in Scarlet" (1887)

Software engineering is an old art.

It is generally known as a branch of engineering that applies programming techniques and languages, design, and basic project management to solve real problems by developing computer software. Its core principles go back as early as the 1990s, yet we can find in history that the incipit of the ideas behind it is even more ancient if we think about, for example, to Ada Lovelace and Charles Babbage:

The Analytical Engine has no pretensions whatever to originate any thing. It can do whatever we know how to order it to perform.

—Ada Lovelace (1842)

© Giuliana Carullo 2020
G. Carullo, *Implementing Effective Code Reviews*,
https://doi.org/10.1007/978-1-4842-6162-0_1

Legend has it that, at that time, developers cried and screamed, running in circles because they were not able to set clear objectives and to deal with customers' expectations.

After several decades, we studied software engineering in all possible facets, while we often keep on crying because of bad code. Even though plenty of literature has been written on how to collect requirements, design code, and implement it, writing good code and maintaining it clean is a process that requires continuous care and attention. In this chapter, we start introducing what can go wrong and what we can do about it. Following a bottom-up approach, we will introduce the basics of software engineering and code reviews and how they link together. Specifically, we will discuss

- Code smells
- Software development life cycle (SDLC)
- Improving quality with code reviews

This will set the base for the book, serving as a first glance to the details in further chapters: from the nitty-gritty code details to general principles and more complex scenarios including security.

Code Smells

The term *code smell* was introduced by Kent Beck back in the 1990s and became more popular with its introduction in Martin Fowler's book, *Refactoring*.[1] A code smell can be defined as "a surface indication that usually corresponds to a deeper problem in the system."[2]

The purpose of sniffing around for code smells is to find areas that can be improved in the code and eventually identify where refactoring is needed. Code smells are all about improving the overall quality of the software or system under development. And this should be done as early as possible. A smell you think is minor now could become your monster after a while. We are trying to prevent our cute baby code monster from growing into a terrifying code monster with 13 asymmetric legs, 4 heads, and gigantic hands and smelling like it did not have a shower.

Bad habits when writing code range from different causes, including human beliefs (such as the excuse that the code does not need to be perfect) to ignoring decades of old good practices and standards, but they all have the same impact: low maintainable and error-prone code.

---

[1] Martin Fowler, *Refactoring*, 2nd ed. (Addison-Wesley, 2018).
[2] https://martinfowler.com/bliki/CodeSmell.html

Even if writing good code is, and always will be, an incremental process and perfection is a unicorn, we cannot use it as an excuse to not put an effort into writing the best code we possibly can in a given context. Code reviews are also a great tool for learning from more experienced programmers; however, it should not be used as an excuse to write—consciously or unconsciously—bad code knowing that someone will eventually fix it later in a review.

Failing is okay, and we all started with not so great code. However, writing good code is also a matter of attitude, not only skills.

Hence, it is important to put more and more effort into improving code quality. This book looks at different aspects of code quality, from using your instincts to smelling the code to more formal approaches to fix defects and remedying them as soon as they emerge.

But why should we care if code is bad if it does the job? Poor code has plenty of negative implications both immediately and in the long term:

1. ***Poor readability***: A code which is not readable is a code that is more difficult to reuse, extend, and evolve.

2. ***Low productivity***: A peer who is unfamiliar with the code will surely take more time to understand what the code is trying to achieve. Furthermore, you might end up spending more time fixing bugs rather than focusing on the core values added by the software you are implementing.

3. ***Bug pollution***: Bugs can grow in size and number when not promptly addressed.

4. ***Delays in releases***: All the defects in the code start to increase, overlap, and mess up the system. Deadlines might be delayed because of bugs you ignored so far.

5. ***Poor maintainability***: The code is difficult to read. Thus, the development process is slowed down by bugs. Furthermore, it is difficult to know how long it will take to implement new functionalities because of other defects in the system.

At a certain point, you might be even tempted to throw everything away and start from scratch. But please stop! That's not the right way, and there is a solution for this; not the Holy Grail, but it will help—a lot!

Software Development Life Cycle

Software development life cycle (SDLC), in simple words, is the process of building software. Figure 1-1 shows the main steps of software development.

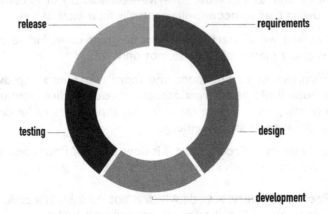

Figure 1-1. Software development life cycle (SDLC)

The **requirements** phase embraces the planning and requirements gathering and analysis processes. The information gathered is used to shape the project in terms of approach, feasibility study, and operational and technical aspects. In this phase, planning for quality of service (QoS) is also performed together with risk identification and their impact. As output of this phase, all the requirements (both functional and nonfunctional) are gathered into the **software requirement specification** (SRS) document.

The **design** phase aims at defining the software architecture, together with coding guidelines, languages, tools, frameworks, and platforms. It starts with the SRS document as input and produces a **design document specification** (DDS) document as output.

The **development** phase aims at actually developing the code accordingly to what has been outlined in the DDS document.

The **testing** phase is, in reality, scattered on the other phases, and it refers to testing the product searching, reporting, monitoring, and fixing defects.

The **release** phase is the ultimate stage where the product is released in the market.

A lot of models have been developed so far. Generally speaking, they describe the order in which each phase of the SDLC is executed. Mainly used models include

- **Waterfall**: In which all the phases are executed in isolation and sequentially. This means that one phase is started only after the previous one is complete.

- **Iterative**: In which the phases are executed sequentially like the waterfall model. However, it starts from a subset of the requirements and the product is iteratively improved until the entire system is implemented.

- **Agile**: Can be seen as an extension of the iterative model, where the entire work is broken down into small, time-constrained tasks, each of them meant to deliver specific features. This model is also incremental, which means that every release is a buildup in terms of features released.

- **Prototype**: Aims at building a small set of product's feature to showcase and evaluate proposals.

Oftentimes, prototypes, by nature, do not focus on performances and security. However, I strongly encourage you to still keep an eye on them and take them into account during the design phase.

Prototypes are also often strongly impacted by the *"ship it fast, that's just a prototype"* mentality. Unfortunately, it implies *"I don't really care about its quality."*

Is this the right way to proceed? My answer is yes and no.

If your prototype takes really little effort to code and mainly runs in isolation, it might be okay to not overstress on its overall quality. However, some of them take months or years to be developed and still called prototypes, with a lot of interactions with other components. Not ensuring good enough quality in this case will surely lead to slowdowns in the development process, which might impact also other components depending on such a low-quality code. A slowdown also means potentially missed deadlines and money.

▨ **Takeaway**   Don't use the SDLC you are embracing to justify how bad smelling the code is. It is surely more harm and time consuming than good.

Figure 1-2 shows the comprehensiveness of solid code reviews and how they fit into the development life cycle. Code reviews are often implemented by means of peer reviews, hence, often focusing on a small piece of code (e.g., a single pull request) at the time. However, code reviews should be approached regularly from a more comprehensive approach spanning all across the SDLC.

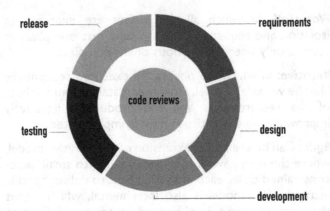

Figure 1-2. Code reviews—SDLC

Improving Quality with Code Reviews

One of the ways I suggest to improve quality is embedding code reviews into the development process.

Code reviews aim at systematically examining the codebase to find defects or potential flaws. Different types of code reviews exist based on the needs of the company and the specific product:

- *Informal reviews* are the more naïve way to check the code for defects. This kind of review usually involves no particular preparation nor planned metrics to measure the effectiveness of the review. They are usually performed by one or more peers, typically for brainstorming ideas.

- *Walkthrough reviews* are slightly more formal than informal reviews. They can be performed by a single person (e.g., the author of the code) or by multiple participants. Defects are usually pointed out and discussed. This type of review is more about querying for feedback and comments from participants rather than actually correcting defects.

- *Inspection reviews* are well planned and structured. It aims at finding and logging defects, gathering insights, and communicating them within the team. The process is supported by a checklist and metrics to gather the effectiveness of the review process. It is usually not performed by the author.

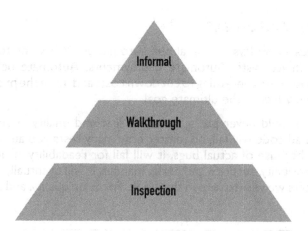

Figure 1-3. Types of code reviews

Of the three types shown in Figure 1-3, code inspection is the most disciplined approach for discovering and correcting defects into the code.

▓ **On Peer Reviews**   Peer reviews are probably the most common way of performing code reviews that you have been going through and that you performed in your engineering career. They do not show in the pyramid because, even if they help in spotting some inconsistencies within the code as well as bugs, achieving clean code cannot be confined to small features, especially with software growing at scale. The guidance provided in this book can surely be applied also to peer reviews. However, the suggestion is to periodically take a step away from small portions of code and look at the code in its broader form and cleanness, hence, the approaches presented in Figure 1-2 and the structure of this book.

Code inspection is a broader review because it focuses on different aspects of code quality, from obvious logic errors including coding standards and style guidelines. And since we care about the quality of the software we produce, this book will focus and provide practical guidance, on this type of review.

▓ **Rule of Thumb**   Reviews should be well integrated into any existing development process, and it should be done fairly early in the development process. As the proverb goes, those who start well are half away from achieving their goal.

Next, we'll introduce manual and automated code reviews and provide a glance at the benefits brought to the table when performing them.

Manual vs. Automated

A lot of times nowadays I hear about automation. We want to automate reviews. Automate tests. Automate deployments. Automate behavior. We just want to automate everything to cut down costs and make the programmer's life a bit easier, which is the ultimate goal.

However, we should never put automation first and quality after. Quality is the priority. Bad code will fail, no matter how many tests you automated. If it does not fail because of actual bugs, it will fail for readability, maintainability, usability, extensibility, security, and performances. It will eventually fail because of all the defects we will explore in this book. Focus on quality, and automation will follow.

■ **Takeaway** Automation is a big friend in our programming life—from automated formatting and styles. It saves a lot of time that otherwise would be wasted for manual repetitive tasks. Automated tests are also a fundamental piece that helps, if done correctly, to quickly spot if any change breaks something else in the codebase. The key takeaway here is: even the best tests can spot breaking changes but will not ensure clean code.

Certain aspects of code reviews can be automated and are often referred to as *static code analysis*. Finding performance issues or a standard violation, as an example, might and should be automatized. However, even if a good rule of thumb is to automatize as much as possible to achieve faster and repeatable processes, you should surely not neglect manual code reviews (hence this book). For instance, as we'll discuss later, long methods are oftentimes the signal that something wrong might be happening: it might be the case of a method implementing more than a single functionality or behavior. In this case, a reviewer needs to look at the actual code to understand if there is a problem or the code is just fine as it is.

Manual reviews performed by experts can provide different benefits including

1. Better insights around the overall quality of the software

2. Less false positive/negatives

3. Clear suggestions on corrective actions to fix defects

4. Prioritizing and clearly defining the risks deriving from defects found

Impact

Code reviews are relatively cheap, especially if you consider the amazing benefits derived from a handful of hours spent in analyzing the code:

1. *Return of investment* (ROI): Code reviews have an amazing return of investment. They not only pay for themselves immediately, but they will keep working and will be cost-effective in the long run. In the short term, resolving defects found will improve how quickly the following features can be implemented. In the long run, the more you keep the code nice and clean, the less time expensive the following reviews will likely be.

2. *Agility*: They fit (very) well agile processes. They allow the development process to fully embrace changes. By iterating reviews, changes, defects discovery, and fixing them, teams are continuously set for success. Ensuring good quality as you keep developing translates into long-term maintainability. The only way for code reviews (quality code in general) and agile not to go hand in hand is if they are looked from the eyes of those who do not have a real grasp of both.

3. *Productivity*: No matter if a defect is a bug (e.g., a logic error you found in the code) or there is a readability issue coming from a not so well-written code, the productivity of the team increases.

4. *Impact on other processes*: Embedding code reviews also positively impacts other processes including testing and refactoring. Furthermore, testing by itself does not ensure quality code. Yes, the functionality might not crack, but there is no assurance that the code is in good shape.

5. *Learning*: Code reviews can be a good learning experience. They don't need to be a boring process—and they are actually not. They really can be a fun way to brainstorm and solve issues.

6. *Lesson learned*: As the code grows and new requirements (functional or nonfunctional) are developed, lesson learned and good insights for future implementations can be gathered.

7. ***Branding***: Releasing good quality code speaks about ourselves and about the company. We can't produce perfect code, but we can put our best effort to be happy about the code we show to the world. At the end of the day, it is not just what you do; it is how you do it.

Summary

In this chapter, we went over the importance of building and maintaining clean code and introduced basic knowledge around software development life cycle. In the next chapters, we will examine each of the phases in the SDLC and see how they can benefit from code reviews. Before continuing, let's summarize the takeaways from this chapter to take with you on your journey to become a better software engineer:

1. Clean code is not only a matter of skills: it's also about having the right attitude. Always put the best effort you can when writing code.

2. Code reviews are not only beneficial during the entire SDLC: they are necessary to maintain clean code over time.

Code Structure

The world is full of obvious things which nobody by any chance ever observes.

—Sherlock Holmes in Sir Arthur Conan Doyle's
"The Hound of the Baskervilles" (1902)

In the early days of programming, being able to create *Turing-complete* algorithms was so innovative that people were not that much concerned with structured programming.

Few years later, in 1968, Edsger W. Dijkstra wrote his open letter "Go To Statement Considered Harmful," where structured programming was born.

Today, structured code represents the very basics of clean code and something to really consider not only from a technical perspective but also for its implication to the economics of writing successful code.

Thus, in this chapter, we will take a closer look at the following aspects and what we should look for when doing code reviews:

- What makes bad code
- Core principles of clean code and good practices
- Dos and don'ts of object-oriented (OO) programming
- Software architectures

G. Carullo, *Implementing Effective Code Reviews*,
https://doi.org/10.1007/978-1-4842-6162-0_2

What Makes Bad Code?

First, let's talk about the worst kind of code: spaghetti code. Much like the noodles it is named after, spaghetti code is limp, unstructured, and can turn into a mess if not controlled. Technically, spaghetti code

- Violates principles of structured code
- Has arbitrary control flows
- Has jumps (back-in-the-day GOTOs) here and there

There are other kinds of "badly written code," but spaghetti code deals with an even more severe problem: bad code structure.

If a codebase is well designed (e.g., modular), bad code can still be spotted and fixed. Spaghetti code—and any other example of badly structured code—requires tedious, often avoided, refactoring. Although it is possible to fix bad code, it is much more difficult to fix spaghetti code. For that reason, in this chapter, we will provide the fundamentals for assembling a nicely layered lasagna instead of ending up with an inextricable tangle of spaghetti.

Note   Unstructured code makes everything so difficult to maintain.

Recipe for Disaster

Even though modern programming languages oftentimes proclaim

> I would rather see you begging for mercy rather than giving you that magic GOTO statement

we can still create our best spaghetti version for lunch.

Refresher   GOTO statements are unconditional jumps from one portion of the code to another. They provide a mean, differently from loops and conditional statements (if-then-else), to unconditionally change the execution flow. As a consequence, they are highly discouraged if the language provides them because they make the flow very difficult to understand and many modern programming languages do not provide GOTO at all.

Let me give you the best recipe for spaghetti code in the world:

- Do not design your solution in advance, that is, no architecture, nothing.

- Use a bunch of global variables.

- Use an object-oriented (OO) language, but dismiss all the benefits (inheritance, polymorphism, etc.).

- Forget that someone told you that design patterns exist. They are your enemy.

- Write big classes with tons of different responsibilities.

- Write highly coupled components.

- Don't think about APIs and just pick and choose your preferred names.

- If parallelization is required, just add a bunch of threads when you think it might somehow work.

- Don't consider code reusability; someone else needs to reinvent the wheel in case needed.

If this recipe makes you cry and there are no onions in the room, you already understand why spaghetti code is bad. So, don't do it! Either way, in the next sections, we will start untangling piece by piece the ingredients of the preceding recipe.

Fundamental Principles of Good Code

Now that we've discussed what not to do, what are we supposed to do? This section introduces the always green principles—the ground truth of clean coding.

The Zen of Python

The "Zen of Python"[1] states the fundamental principles that every programmer should follow. It is as follows:

Beautiful is better than ugly.

Explicit is better than implicit.

---

[1]www.python.org/dev/peps/pep-0020/

Simple is better than complex.

Complex is better than complicated.

Flat is better than nested.

Sparse is better than dense.

Readability counts.

Special cases aren't special enough to break the rules.

Although practicality beats purity.

Errors should never pass silently.

Unless explicitly silenced.

In the face of ambiguity, refuse the temptation to guess.

There should be one– and preferably only one –obvious way to do it.

Although that way may not be obvious at first unless you're Dutch.

Now is better than never.

Although never is often better than right now.

If the implementation is hard to explain, it's a bad idea.

If the implementation is easy to explain, it may be a good idea.

Namespaces are one honking great idea – let's do more of those!

It is a pleasure to see how beautifully and simply the *Zen of Python* states its core design principles behind the language. And it also provides a solid base for engineering any code that you will type using it.

■ **Note** Even if the Zen of Python, as the name says, describes the guiding principles behind Python, it is and should be used as a good summary of guiding principles for any code in any language.

KISS Principle

The KISS principle stands for **keep it simple stupid**. The underlying idea is to keep the code as simple as possible so that it will be easier to work on it later.

Complex or complicated code takes longer to design, write, and test. And it might be harder to modify or maintain in the future.

I would still avoid, however, being "cheap" during design phase. Simple is far better, but missing core requirements and not embedding them into the process is as detrimental as overcomplicating things.

If you don't understand your code well enough to write it into its most simple version, how can you look back at the code and get what it was supposed to do in the future?

■ **Note** Some programmers might be tempted to write complex code for the sake of showing their mastery of the language. Meanwhile, certain feature of a given language might suit your code, be always aware if any other version would make it simpler.

Reusability

Let me tell you a story. In 1812, Charles Babbage came up with the idea that computation could be performed by a fast reliable machine. He called this machine the *Analytical Engine*. In the following years, Ada Lovelace described an algorithm for this engine able to compute Bernoulli numbers. Thus, the first program was born.

Even back then, the wise Ada already understood the wisdom of having reusable code. She actually recognized that the machine

> Was not a mere steampunk abacus, but a device that can process data of any kind, and perhaps even reason.

Reusability is an innate concept; why do we persist in neglecting it in our code so often?

Code reusability aims at saving time, money, and resources by eliminating unneeded redundancy by designing the code in a way that once created, it can be used in some shape or form by other components during the software development process.

Think about not having reusable code. It's like constantly asking a machine that is able to reason to think about the exact same issue and solve it over and over. It's not a proper use of such a capable resource.

If I have not convinced you yet, duplication is definitely tedious to deal with. Do you enjoy books that have the same concept repeated over and over? I bet you do not. And, even if in books repetition can still have the purpose of acting as a reminder (up to an extent), in programming the other way around is a recipe for disaster.

In conclusion, avoid repetition at all costs: it leads to high levels of coupling and makes the code less performant and more difficult to read.

Takeaway   Writing reusable code is a cornerstone of clean code. If the code duplicates logic and/or data, it is breaking this principle.

Readability

Good readability means that it takes little time to understand what a piece of code is doing.

Human brain is so complex, but we all still forget things. Can you remember complex, long, and random passwords? No way. Maybe only one if you repeat it every day.

What chance do you have to quickly remember a random name of a variable and get the context in which it has been used?

Naming and proper commenting are one facet of readability, which will be addressed in the majority of the proposed good practices presented in this book.

Facts from the World   In 1956, the psychologist George Miller suggested that human capacity to remember items in the short term is limited somewhere between five and seven items. How many lines of code (LOCs) do we professionally write every day? How many variables? Definitely more than five every day. Help your memory by embedding context. This would benefit readability too.

Other important aspects of a well-flowing (i.e., readable) code include

- Indentation
- Following the guidelines from the given programming language to implicitly express intentions (e.g., declaring a private variable or a global one)

- Functions, methods, and classes are short and on point
- Maintaining consistent conventions across the entire codebase (e.g., single quotes vs. double quotes)

All these aspects of readable code will, of course, be analyzed more in depth in the remainder of this book.

Modularity

Modularity is a basic principle of software systems. It means that components in a software system should be cohesive and loosely coupled.

A **cohesive** component has a clearly defined function. Multiple components are **loosely coupled** if the dependencies between each other are minimal.

In general terms, modularity is applied every time we get to decide which portion of code goes into which function, module, class, or package.

This principle impacts on several *quality attributes* including

- Readability due to the logical split of code.
- Modular code consists of well-separated components. In such case, modifying one component would have minimal impact on others.
- By tightening together logically cohesive pieces of code, reusability increases.

■ **Takeaway**   Modular code is easier to maintain and refactor. Always look for logic that can be generalized, put in its own component, and reused elsewhere in the code.

Maintainability

Maintainability is generally used to refer to how easy it is to maintain code over time.

It involves

- How easy will it be to extend the code in the future (**extensibility**)?
- How easy will it be to rework or refactor the code?

A lot of principles and quality aspects impact on this very broad definition. As an example, not easily readable code makes the code harder to understand

and, hence, to modify later on during the development process. As you saw in the previous section, also modularity contributes to an overall easy-to-maintain code.

■ **Note** As tempting as it is to provide quick and hot fixes for bugs in the code, especially if on a strict deadline, always go for looking at the root cause of the issue at hand. This would greatly benefit how easy to maintain code in the long run (and also the likelihood of not having to fix a bug several times).

Testability

Testability refers to how easy it is to ensure correctness of code by means of writing tests for it.

Clean code allows not only for easier bug discovery but also for easier times when writing testing code and procedures.

Readability plays a very important role in testing a piece of software. A generally good practice is to have a developer and a tester to be two different people in order to ensure. The rationale behind is similar to writing a book. Proofreading and editing is normally performed by a person different from the author. Indeed, for the author, it might be easier to neglect mistakes (e.g., typos) since they already know what's written. This guideline is even more true in industrial settings at scale. In such cases, indeed, often, yet not always, different specialized roles are in place: developer and tester. In such case, having readable code helps the tester to quickly and better understand what to test for.

■ **Note** Testability goes well beyond code readability. It is highly encouraged communication between developers and testers to ensure that requirements and scope are clear to both in order to drive what cases need to be tested. The more the knowledge and understanding of the software under testing, the better the outcome.

Understandably, not all the companies have the same processes in place, and you might find yourself being both the programmer and the test writer of a single feature. It would be not the end of the world, and I am sure if you are in such conditions you'd be great anyway with the results!

However, if more than one person is in the team, an encouraged practice would still be to add a different perspective to who does and/or reviews the tests.

Composition vs. Inheritance

▨ **Refresher**   Composition and inheritance are two techniques used to establish relationships between components. The first, as the name says, allows relationships to be created by putting and using together multiple components. As an example, a car can be seen as a composition of wheels, engine, windows, sets, and so on. The latter allows for extending the behavior of an object. For example, a dog can be seen as a general extension of the abstraction animal.

The composition vs. inheritance principle means that to achieve polymorphism, composition should be preferred instead of inheritance.

Composition usually presents a more flexible design, thus resulting in being maintainable in the long run. Not only are designs based on composition easier to write; they will also accommodate future requirements and changes without requiring a complete restructuring of the hierarchy.

Truth to be told, composition comes with minor drawbacks including *forwarding methods*. This happens when the behavior of the *composer* for a certain method needs to match the behavior of the composed object. In this case, the composer only needs to call the relative method from the composed object.

As a rule of thumb, if too many *forwarding methods* are in the code, they may signal the—very few—cases where inheritance might be preferred in the current design. In this case, just reevaluate it.

Premature Optimization

The *premature optimization* principle suggests that you resist the urge of speed up before it is necessary.

Again, being cautious with not writing unneeded code as well as unneeded optimizations does not mean being "cheap" with design. Parallelizing your newborn code might be unneeded, hence totally embrace this principle. However, do not use it as an excuse to write bad code by not considering performance requirements.

As an example, suppose that you are building a new framework and that a functionality running on top of it needs to match a 100ms runtime mark. Sure enough you have to consider it and not only for the algorithm behind the actual functionality. The framework's design should be designed in such a way to make the goal actually achievable.

These principles are inherently anti-spaghetti code, so following them will help you write better code. Now, let's look at the bigger picture.

■ **Takeaway**   Proper design and premature optimization are not the same thing. Always strive for good design, and leave premature optimization for later during the implementation process.

Sound Software Architectures

Truth to be told, there is no single path to write perfect code. Good-design and sound software architectures are the inceptions to write better software.

Software architectures constitute the very first step to write marvelous code. The kind of code you don't hate to read. The kind of code you don't hate to troubleshoot, to extend... Okay, you got the point.

We love to code and to dig deep into the latest cool technology. But the shiniest tech would not help us—by itself—to achieve our goal: make others love the quality of the code we write. We may have unconditional love for our cute code babies—no matter how well (or bad) they are written. But others won't necessarily love them: the harsh truth. So, we need to raise our code babies right so they can be outstanding members of a strong software architecture.

There are a few things you can do to make sure you have a good software architecture that will get the job done and will make others love the quality of your code.

We will expand on what it means to have a sound software architecture and what to look for during reviews in Chapter 5.

Be People Minded

One of the best things about writing quality code is that it will make people happy: colleagues, stakeholders, and customers, you name it. Everyone will be happier; even your mom will pat you on your shoulder, believe me. And this is one of the most critical points for engineers in today's tech jobs: how well you serve your audience. Writing good quality code is—for sure—rewarding, but our main job is to serve others, to which extent we improve their lives.

Software architectures help in driving this major success goal. Good architectures are not only linked to applying design patterns, designing APIs, and optimizing performances (which would make your colleagues happy). It is also about finding the right trade-offs between maintainability, usability, security, and any other requirements both internal (the company you work for) and external (stakeholders' interests).

■ **Note**   As engineers, we like programming and we are with high likelihood industrious people: we like to build and create things. However the human element cannot be removed from our creations: anything we do is meant to serve someone else, not writing beautiful code alone.

The biggest recommendation that I can give you to this regard is to always approach any piece of code from three different angles:

- Customer driven
- Data driven
- Engineering driven

Neglecting any of them will eventually provide some results, but not the best the code can achieve.

We already started thinking about how important it is to implement something that is really needed and solves the right problem. However, any problem which, for example, lacks of the data-driven perspective might limit the opportunities to add even more value on top of the current customers' needs. At the same time, having a customer-driven approach without proper engineering supporting the code (and hence clean code) causes bugs and errors to pave their way up to the customers and, possibly, missing deadlines because of improper processes and development effort.

Au contraire, the best tools and data exploration will serve no purpose if the result is not what the customer wanted, or if the proposal is not perceived as valued.

Be SMART

Oftentimes, the counting lines of code (LOCs) are used to gauge project "quality." But we really need to go a step further. Nope, 100k LOCs of code do not necessarily mean the project is more complex—or better—than 50k LOCs. I think that the quality of the code reflects more on the architecture. And it serves us better to be *SMART,* which stands for being specific, measurable, achievable/realistic, and time-bound. By following this guide, our architecture will be **s**pecific to requirements; **m**easurable in terms of usability, maintainability, performances, and so on; **a**chievable/**r**ealistic (simple is often better), **t**ime-bound (which would make others also happy).

Once again, a well-designed software architecture is the primary need for a good start. Bad code happens; bad architectures are the enemy. Architectures provide needed boundaries for the code to be developed. And they help—a lot—in avoiding modern spaghetti code.

If you are dealing with spaghetti code:

- Set standards that the code will follow
- Embrace good practices
- Design the API and stick to it
- Refactor the code

And do it as soon as possible; a small short-term investment will work wonder in the long run. Don't strive for perfection—less than optimal code might also work depending on business needs. But don't neglect architectures. Writing good code or improving it as we go seems not worthy initially, but it will definitely pay off at the end.

■ **Note** Always leave the code in a better shape than the one you found.

APIs

Let's look at another recipe for disaster: API (application programming interface) spaghetti omelet. For this recipe, you will need

- Spaghetti code
- Beaten API eggs
- A grain of salt

The preparation is fairly simple: Get the spaghetti you already have. Grab your best engineer and make him/her beat eggs for a couple of minutes. Eggs' volume will increase, and the texture starts to get thicker and foamy (spaghetti already starts to appear tastier). Mix all together and use a grain of salt for flavor. Deep fry, and serve while still hot.

You might think that spaghetti code can be reasonable because at least APIs are clearly defined and "only" the code is messed up.

> ■ **Note**   Any layer of complexity you add is one more layer of potentially new weaknesses popping into the products you are building. A famous security principle states that the security of a chain is as strong as the security of its weakest link. The same can easily be ported to clean code: a code is as much clean as its least clean piece of software.

On the other end, building a solid API requires as much care as any other piece of software. As an example, error handling is very critical for APIs too. A common mistake is to think about error handling later in the development process. And it can easily become too late, potentially leaving who calls the API confused about the response they get (if human calling up).

Error handling, as well as the format of the response, should be clear, documented, and uniform across the code. In such way, any automation process on top of the API will be easier, quicker, and cleaner.

The API-first approach has become fairly popular in recent years to help with the design of consistent and clean API. As the name suggests, such approach consists of prioritizing the design of APIs establishing rules and agreements on how the given application is supposed to behave. This approach responds generally well to scenarios where there is a need for customer to interact with the application (e.g., by means of mobile, tablets, and websites).

Even if this approach might not suit every development process, it still has some beneficial concepts and implication that come with it that you should include when thinking of APIs:

- It provides a very useful perspective on what the software is meant to do.

- It helps to consider edge cases.

- It helps in isolating logical problems, hence providing a possibly more structured approach to their resolution.

We will further explore the need for thinking about the broader problem in Chapter 6. However, the main takeaway for this section is as follows:

- Do not hide dirty code under the API carpet.

- Do not underestimate the importance of the APIs and their consistency.

- When writing code, especially if the mind starts to wonder, call it back and think about what the problem you are really trying to solve is.

Be Mindful of Control Structures

GOTOs are not the only way of altering control flows. Some attention needs to be put also in more innocuous *if-then-else* statements.

This construct surely will not harm readability as GOTOs. However, having completely defined constructs is needed to both improve readability and have the certainty of a well-defined code behavior. Completely defined means having an else-for-each-if statement.

Pay Attention to Health Status

Looking at the code quality goes beyond defects. Here are five health indicators to consider in order to avoid spaghetti architectures:

1. **Problem definition**: Everything starts with the problem definition. An unclear or not completely defined problem will surely lead to cluttered and bad smelling architectures and even worst code. Ensure that the overall problem that needs to be solved is clearly defined, what is in scope and what is not, and—when applicable—that a minimum viable product (MVP) and a road map to achieve it are defined and communicated.

2. **Validate the architecture**: The solution might be relatively fancy but won't solve the problem. Take some time to go through requirements (functional and nonfunctional) to validate the proposed design.

3. **Rethink technologies**: Languages, tools, platforms, and frameworks need to be considered based on overall requirements. Don't follow the approach "if all you have is a hammer, everything looks like a nail."

4. **Knowledge**: As part of reaching the best possible product, human aspects also need to be considered. Does the team have proper domain knowledge? If not, training in all shapes and forms is the way to go. But once again, don't look at everything as a nail.

5. **Processes**: Even the best team, with a well-rounded architecture, can't work in the most productive way if there are no systematic processes to follow in order to obtain a manageable development.

Summary

Ensuring code quality is broader than what it seems. It is not just having good code, nor is it only about having good architectures.

As explained in this chapter

1. Evaluating status and potential risks around the highlighted indicators should be part of our continuous review process.

2. Pairing code and architecture reviews with an overall health status will help products to be on track and achieve their best shapes.

3. Hiding unclean code under the carpet (APIs or any form of wrappers) does not solve the issue.

In the next chapter, we will start digging deeper at how we can add reviews at design phase and what we need to look at in order to maintain sound structure, behavior, and dependencies across the entire codebase.

Code Review Checklist

The following are potential structure issues that should be checked during code review:

1. Does the actual implementation reflect the architecture?
2. Is the code easy to understand?
3. Is the code too long?
4. Is cohesion in place?
5. Is the code modular?
6. Are components cohesive?
7. Is the code loosely coupled?
8. Is the code reusable?
9. Is the code readable?
10. Is the code easy to maintain and test?
11. Are premature optimizations in place?
12. Is composition preferred?
13. Is inheritance properly used?

14. Is the flow easy to understand?

15. Are interactions between different components easy to catch?

16. Are conditional flows completely defined?

17. Is there any undefined behavior?

18. Are APIs consistent and as clean as the overall code?

Data Structures

It is a capital mistake to theorize before one has data. Insensibly one begins to twist facts to suit theories, instead of theories to suit facts.

—Sherlock Holmes, "A Study in Scarlet" (1877)

Data structures are often not analyzed as carefully as a software architecture would have been, but they definitely have their spot on the stage. Choosing them correctly has a lot of benefits, including

- Readability since the wrong data structures can make the code more complex than what actually required.

- Better design because they are strictly related to project's *requirements*:

    - How data can be better organized?

    - How to improve performances?

    - Are there any memory constraints?

- Fun: yes, you'll have a lot of fun with them.

In this chapter, we will introduce common data structures and how to evaluate them in the overall grand scheme of designing clean code.

© Giuliana Carullo 2020
G. Carullo, *Implementing Effective Code Reviews*,
https://doi.org/10.1007/978-1-4842-6162-0_3

Introduction to Data Structures

Table 3-1 shows some of the main data structures with relative average time complexity for basic operation (i.e., access, insert, delete, search).

Table 3-1. Time Complexity

Data Structure	Access	Insert	Delete	Search
Array	O(1)	O(n)	O(n)	O(n)
Linked list	O(n)	O(1)	O(1)	O(n)
Doubly linked list	O(n)	O(1)	O(1)	O(n)
Queue	O(n)	O(1)	O(1)	O(n)
Stack	O(n)	O(1)	O(1)	O(n)
Hash map	Constant (avg)	O(1)	O(1)	O(1)
Binary search tree	O(n log n)	O(n log n)	O(n log n)	O(n log n)

Taking into account the performances of a given data structure should not be an afterthought. And it matches well the good-design way of proceeding. The more suitable the data structures, the more optimized, effective, and efficient the design is.

■ **Refresher** Asymptotic analysis (as shown in Table 3-1) allows to express time performances in the context of the size of the data (i.e., the number of elements). In short, if an operation always takes the "same" amount of time (i.e., not dependent on the size of the data), we say that it has constant time and we refer to it as O(1). If an operation scales logarithmically with the data size, we refer to it as O(log n). If an operation scales linearly with the data size, we say that it runs in linear time and we refer to it as O(n). Operations can also scale in polynomial (e.g., O(n2)) and exponential (e.g., O(2n)) time. Always try to understand if and how polynomial and exponential operations can be optimized.

Some indicators that can be used to evaluate which data structure is appropriate or not are

- Data size
- Does the data changes and how often?
- Are search and sorting operation frequent?

Note When reasoning around data size, do not focus only on the problem at hand. Try to look at possible future cases and how data might possibly scale over time. This would help not only in considering data in the context at hand but also spotting any limiting or better options in terms of runtime.

A very well-known principle, which can be applied to data structure as well, is the Pareto principle, also known as the 80/20 principle. This principle states that 20% of causes generate 80% of the results.

As you will read in the rest of the chapter, every data structure comes not only with a general context that might suit them better. They also come with different runtimes for common operation (e.g., adding and deleting elements). To pick and validate data structure, one of the approaches you can explore is to think about the 80% of operations that you need to perform on a given set of data and evaluate which data structure would be the most performant (runtime) data structure to use in such context.

Pareto Example Consider a scenario where 80% of operations are given by adding and searching elements in a data structure. As from Table 3-1, you can start confronting time complexity. Would it be optimal to use a linked list with $O(n)$ search? Definitely not. By using HashMaps, you could have a better running time since by design HashMaps suit really good searching operations with a constant average runtime.

Let's go through the pros and cons of each data structure.

Array

The array data structure is probably the simplest one. It is a collection of elements that can be accessed by means of *indexes*. Arrays can be **linear** (i.e., single dimension) or **multidimensional** (e.g., matrixes). Figure 3-1 shows a representation of this data structure of size n.

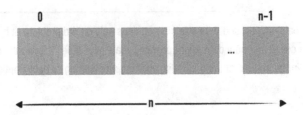

Figure 3-1. Array

■ **Refresher**   Each box in Figure 3-1 represents an element within the array, each of which with a relative position within the array. Position counting always starts at 0.

Basic arrays are fixed in size, which is the size declared during initialization. They support only a single type (e.g., all integers).

In Python, array declaration can be performed as

```
from array import *
a = array('i', [1,2,3])
```

where the first parameter 'i' specifies the *typecode*, which in the specific case refers to signed integers of 2 bytes. The second parameter provides initializers for the given array.

Some languages support dynamic sizing as well as different data types. It is the case, for example, of Python where the following code will be fine:

```
array = [1, "string", 0.2]
```

and all the types are properly managed:

```
type(array[0])
>>> <type 'int'>

type(array[1])
>>> <type 'str'>

type(array[2])
>>> <type 'float'>
```

■ **Note**   As you might have noted already from the first snippet of code, the array requires the import of the standard module "array." This is because Python does not natively support arrays. Other libraries, including NumPy, also provide their own implementation of arrays. However, it is pretty common to use Python lists in day-to-day code instead of arrays due to their flexibility.

They come with several pros and cons.

They are fairly easy to use and—as shown in Table 3-1—they provide direct access by means of *indexes*, and the entire list of elements can be accessed linearly in $O(n)$, where n is the number of elements into the list.

However, inserting and deleting items from the list are more computationally expensive due to shifting operation required to perform these operations. As a worst-case scenario, to better understand why it happens, consider deleting the first element of the list which is at index = 0. This operation creates an empty spot; thus all the items from index = 1 need to be shifted one position backward. This gives us a complexity of $O(n)$. Analogous considerations are for insertion.

Linked List

A linked list is a collection of nodes, where each node is composed of a *value* and a *pointer* to the next node into the list (Figure 3-2).

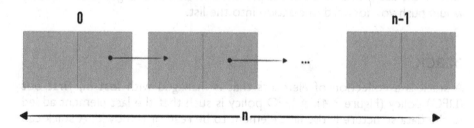

Figure 3-2. Linked list

Compared to arrays, *add* and *remove* operations are easier because no shifting is required. Removing an item from the list can be performed by changing the pointer of the element prior to the one that needs to be removed. Time complexity is still $O(n)$ in the worst case. Indeed, in order to find the item that needs to be removed, it is required to navigate the entire list up to the searched element. The worst case happens when the removal needs to be done on the last element into the list. Often linked lists serve well as underlying implementation of other data structures including stacks and queues.

Doubly Linked List

A doubly linked list is similar to regular linked lists, but each node stores a pointer to the previous node in the list (Figure 3-3).

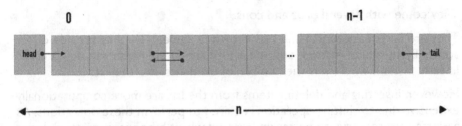

Figure 3-3. Doubly linked list

Adding is slightly more complex than the previous type due to more pointers to be updated. *Add* and *remove* operations still take *O(n)* due to sequential access needed to locate the right node. In a figurative way, think about this doubly linked list as the navigation bar into your Google search. You have the current page (the node) and two links (pointers) to the previous and following page. Another example is the command history. Suppose you are editing a document. Each action you perform on the text (type text, erase, add image) can be considered a node which is added to the list. If you click the undo button, the list would move to the previous version of changes. Clicking redo would push you forward one action into the list.

Stack

A stack is a collection of elements that is managed with *last in, first out* (LIFO) policy (Figure 3-4). A LIFO policy is such that the last element added to the data structure is the first element to be read or removed. A stack can be implemented either with arrays or linked lists.

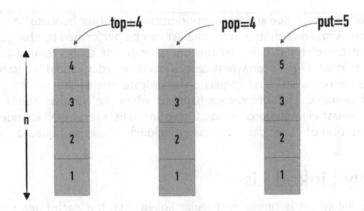

Figure 3-4. Stack

It provides three main methods:

1. **Top( )**: Which returns the element on top of the stack
2. **Pop( )**: Which removes the element on top and returns it
3. **Put( )**: Which adds a new element on top of the stack

It suits well certain categories of problems including pattern validation (e.g., well-parenthesized expressions) as well as general parsing problems due to the LIFO policy.

Queue

A queue is a collection of elements that is managed with *first in, first out* (FIFO) policy (Figure 3-5). A FIFO policy is such that the first element added to the data structure is also the first element read or removed. Similar to stacks, it can be implemented either with arrays or linked lists.

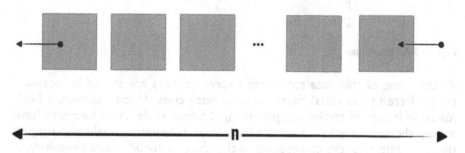

Figure 3-5. Queue

It provides three main methods:

1. **Peak( )**: Which returns the first element in the queue
2. **Remove( )**: Which removes the first element and returns it
3. **Add( )**: Which adds a new element at the end of the queue

Queues are commonly used in concurrent scenarios, where several tasks need to be processed or for messaging management. Generally, queues can be used when order preservation is needed, hence problems that benefit from a FIFO approach. As an example, queues see common usage in cases where asynchronous messages are sent to a single point from different sources to a single processing point. In this scenario, queues are used for synchronization purposes. A real-world case of queue utilization is a printer, both shared (e.g., office printer) and personal. In both cases, multiple file can be sent simultaneously to the printer. However, the printer will queue them depending on arrival and will serve them in arrival time order (the first file to arrive is the first file to be printed).

Hash Map

Hash maps store data as (key, values) pairs (Figure 3-6). Main operations (insert, delete, and lookup) run in $O(1)$ time in the average case.

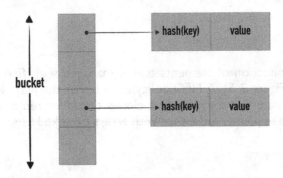

Figure 3-6. Hash map

As the name of this data structures expresses, keys are stored in locations (also referred to as **slots**) based on their **hash code**. Upon insertion, a **hash function** is applied to the key, producing the hash code. Hash functions have to map the same key into the same hash code. However, it might also happen that two different keys correspond to the same hash code, hence resulting in a **collision**. A good hash function is meant to minimize collisions.

The runtime strictly depends on the strength of the hash function to uniformly spread objects across the **bucket** (generally represented as an array of keys).

Being pragmatic, hash maps have really good performances in real-world scenarios. An example of utilization is the phone agenda. Indeed, for every friend you have (keys), a phone number is attached to it (values). Every time you want to call a specific friend, you perform a search (lookout) of their name (key) and you get the relative phone number (value).

A common error that can happen when using this data structure is trying to modify the key element into the data structure. In such case, it might be that this data structure does not suit the problem you are trying to solve.

As an example, consider the following hash map:

```
names = {"Harry": "Potter"}
```

If instead of maintaining the key stable (i.e., Harry) and just updating the value of the entry (i.e., from Potter to a different surname), you are trying to imagine this data structure as being able to change the same entry into "James Potter," you probably need to better think the problem and use a different data structure.

Binary Search Trees

Trees are other fairly commonly used data structures. A tree is a collection of elements, where each element has a *value* and an arbitrary number of *pointers* to other nodes (namely, *children*).

They are organized in a *top-down* fashion, meaning that pointers usually link nodes *up* to *bottom* and each node has a single pointer referencing to it. The first node in this data structure is called the **root** of the tree. Nodes with no children are the **leaves** of the tree. The leaves of the tree are also referred to as the frontier of the tree.

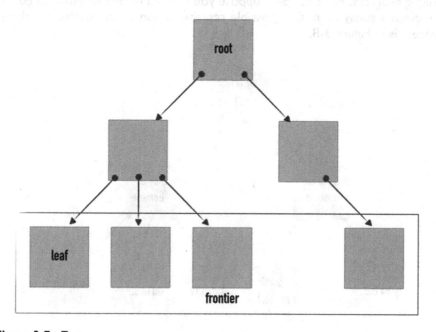

Figure 3-7. Tree

Figure 3-7 shows an example of tree, where the top node (root) has two child nodes. The left child in turn has three children, while the root's right has only one.

Trees are used every time we need to represent a hierarchical organization. Several use cases require a particular type of tree: **binary tree**. In this case, each node has at most two children, namely, **left** and **right**. Even more specifically, its ordered version is even more interesting: the **binary search tree** is used. Each node in the tree is maintained in such a way that, for each node,

- The left child's value is less than or equal to the node's value.

- The right child's value is greater than or equal to the node's value.

The main benefit of this type of tree is that it enables a fast element search. Indeed, due to the ordering, each time half of the tree is excluded from the search (in the average case). As a consequence, binary search trees see sorting problems as one of their main applications.

In general, problems that can be easily solved **recursively** can benefit from trees. In real-world use case, trees can be used to represent any decision-making progress. For example, suppose you have to decide whether to go to the cinema today or not. A possible representation of the decision-making process is in Figure 3-8.

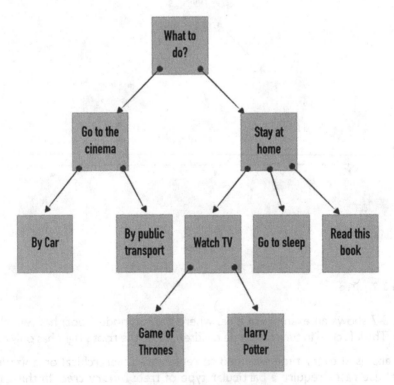

Figure 3-8. Example of decision making using a tree representation

Every node in the example represents incrementally (top to bottom) alternatives at hand. By walking down the tree, indeed, you might decide that you are not going to the cinema, hence staying at home, and that you will watch TV, specifically *Game of Thrones*.

▇ **Spoiler Alert**   Options other than "Read this book" are an act of kindness from the author. Hope you are enjoying it so far!

Guidelines on Data Structures

Picking the appropriate data structure will become an innate capability as you keep developing code and as you expand your knowledge on the topic.

The following are some of the key drivers that can help you in navigating the options available:

1. ***Operations***: Always start from the problem you are trying to solve. Which operations do you need to perform? Traversal? Search? Simple addition and removal? Do you need to be able to gather minimum or maximum of a given dataset?

2. ***Ordering and sorting***: Does your data scream for prioritization or any type of sorting of elements? FIFO? LIFO? Does the order need to be preserved? Does the data structure need to automatically handle data sorting?

3. ***Uniqueness***: Does your data require elements into the data structure to appear only once? There are data structures like sets that allow you to reflect uniqueness conditions.

4. ***Relationship between elements***: Does the data fit a hierarchical logical representation? Is the data more linear in nature? Do you need to logically group elements in a more complex way? This is the case, for example, where for each document, you want to be able to track for each word the number of occurrences of that word.

5. **Memory and time performances**: As we seen in this chapter, every data structure has its own memory and time performances. The algorithms you are building on top of the data structure are heavily influenced by the performances of the operations you perform on data. The performance requirements you want to achieve are another key driver for exploring and filtering which data structure suits your needs.

6. **Complexity**: If more than one data structure after all the filtering looks like a fit for purpose, opt for the most simple one.

By applying these criteria, you should be able to both better understand the problem and filter out data structures that do not suit your data and the context it is used in.

Design Use Case

Let's analyze the example from the stack section: analyzing a sequence to ensure it is well parenthesized. In other words, we want to check that [()]() [()] is a correct way of using parenthesis, while [()](is not. And we want to pick the right data structure that supports the problem we are trying to solve.

Based on the drivers, we can see that

1. We do not need complex operation: insertion and removal are all we need.

2. It requires order preservation but no sorting capabilities.

3. Elements are not unique.

4. The problem is linear.

5. The problem can be solved in linear time and memory.

And there is one data structure that suits the needs which is, as anticipated, the stack.

By being one of the simplest data structures available, we can also conclude that stacks are appropriate since we cannot simplify further given the requirements of the problem at hand.

Evaluation and Review

The same driving criteria can and should be applied during reviews. Let's consider the example of counting occurrences of a given word in a text. In other words

> *I love data structures. I promise that I will carefully consider them in my code reviews.*

has an output

I: 3, love: 1, data: 1, structures: 1, promise: 1, that: 1, will: 1, carefully:1, consider: 1, them: 1, in: 1, my:1, code: 1, reviews:1.

The solution you find in the code is to save the sentence as an array:

```
sentence = ["I", "love", "data", "structures", "I", "promise", "that", "I",
"will", "carefully", "consider", "them", "in", "my", "code", "reviews"]
```

and a list for storing the counting of occurrences:

occurrences=[]

A simple algorithm would be

1. For every word in the array (left to right)
    a. Initialize the relative element in the occurrences list with 1
    b. Scan the remaining array
    c. Every time the same word is found, update the relative entry into the occurrences list (i.e., increment of one)
    d. Move to the next element (i.e., word) into the sentence array

Since for every word (n elements), we have to scan the remainder of the array (of size n), the time complexity is $O(n^2)$.

If we analyze the root problem a bit more carefully, we can quickly figure out that the main problem we are trying to solve is a search operation. This is our first red flag: arrays can be used but are not notoriously known for their search capabilities.

Ordering and sorting are not key elements in our problem: no matter what the order is, the result is not impacted by it. Arrays are okay in this regard.

The data is linear in nature, so arrays might fit.

Relationships between elements are our second red flag: we are using two separate data structures, but there is a strict relationship between each word in the sentence and relative counting.

Performance is another red flag; we don't really like linear problems with polynomial time, don't we?

Finally, we may assert that there is nothing more simple than arrays. And that would be true. This is a clear case where we might need to evaluate adding a tiny bit of complexity to get rid of the red flags. If well designed, the solution should not have been made that far.

And the king of optimized search able to express coupling relationship between elements is our dear hash map.

You can now implement changes accordingly. Interestingly enough, if you compare both solutions, the one using hash maps is also simpler and more readable.

■ **Heads Up**   The same approach can be applied to any programming interview you will face. More often than not, they do require implementing some sort of algorithm around data structure.

Summary

This chapter on data structures is not meant to be a data structure book. It aimed at doing a quick refresh on those you'll end up using more often than not. At the end of the day, reviewing data structures is all about fit for purpose, not overcomplicating the code and considering the appropriate one in terms of memory and time performances.

Some rules of thumb when evaluating which data structure to use are

1. If you are trying to force the data structure to do operations that are not natively supported, it might not be the right one for your purpose.

2. Even if the choice of data structure is surely related to the current problem you are trying to solve (e.g., data size), have a vision for possible growth and how it might impact the software.

3. Use the 80/20 Pareto principle to help you choose the best data structure.

4. Don't opt for fancy data structures just for the sake of it. More complex data structure still requires some more memory management and processing. Always strive for a balance between scalability requirements and complexity. Simple is better, but it needs to get the job done.

In the next chapter, we will tackle code smells, what they are, and why they are bad for clean code and provide guidance on how to spot them in your software.

Further Reading

I love data structures. And amazing books are out there that dig deeper into various data structures and algorithms in general. At the top of my list is *Introduction to Algorithms* by Thomas H. Cormen (MIT Press, 2009). It is a must-read if you haven't read it yet.

Code Review Checklist

1. Are data structures appropriately used?

2. Is the data structure appropriate based on the data size the code is dealing with?

3. Are potential changes to data size considered and handled?

4. Is the data structured forced to do operations not natively supported?

5. Does the data structure support growth (i.e., scalability)?

6. Does the data structure reflect the need for relationships between elements?

7. Does the data structure optimally support the operations you need to perform on it?

8. Is the choice of a specific data structure overcomplicating the code?

9. Is the data structure chosen based on most frequent operations to be performed on data?

10. Are you using stacks for problems that do not require FIFO?

11. Are you using queues for problems that do not require LIFO?

12. Does the data structure reflect any ordering on sorting requirements?

13. From a logical perspective, is the code meant to update the key within a hash map? If so, rethink the problem and see if hash maps are the best data structure to deal with it.

Design Smells

I think that there are certain crimes which the law cannot touch, and which therefore, to some extent, justify private revenge.

—Sherlock Holmes in Sir Arthur Conan Doyle's
"The Adventure of Charles Augustus Milverton" (1904)

Not sure if Doyle was thinking about code smells as a crime, but in my opinion it might!

Code reviews are useful in finding defects in portions of code (i.e., a method or a class). However, you have to remember that the code design and architecture can smell, too. Reviewing the architecture aims at considering bigger chunks of code and interactions between components. It is important to evaluate and refactor design and architecture in order to reduce architecture debt.[1] Architectures that are not well designed and/or not properly maintained over time make new functionalities more difficult to develop. Furthermore, technical debt can quickly pile up in such scenario.

---

[1] Ipek Ozkaya (2016). Strategic Management of Architectural Technical Debt. SEI Agile Blog. https://insights.sei.cmu.edu/sei_blog/2012/07/strategic-management-of-architectural-technical-debt.html

© Giuliana Carullo 2020
G. Carullo, *Implementing Effective Code Reviews*,
https://doi.org/10.1007/978-1-4842-6162-0_4

Refresher Technical debt generally refers to any known improvement or not clean code that you left behind, eventually favoring the development of new features. This also includes bugs that you neglect to fix or for which a quick and not so clean workaround is implemented. Architecture debt is any defect at architecture level. These defects are at a higher granularity level than bugs by means of looking at components and their interactions instead of single bits and pieces of code.

The following lists the top eight design smells:

1. **Cyclic dependencies**: A cyclic dependency, also known as *circular dependency*, happens when two—or more—components depend on each other.

2. **Feature density**: This defect happens when a component implements more than a single functionality.

3. **Unstable dependency**: It happens if a component depends on a less stable one.

4. **Mashed components**: As the opposite of the feature density defect, a mashed component is one that should logically be a single functionality, but is scattered on different places in the code.

5. **Ambiguous interface**: Application programming interfaces (APIs) should be extensible and flexible, not unclear or ambiguous.

6. **Mesh components**: This is the case where components are heavily coupled, with a lot of dependencies and oftentimes without clear and well-defined patterns.

7. **First lady components**: This kind of component will do all the possible jobs by itself. It reaches such a growth that it becomes really expensive to maintain.

8. **That's not my responsibility component or bossy component**: At the opposite end of the first lady component, this component likes to delegate stuff that it doesn't want to deal with to other components. The bossy component is not nice to have in code, and oftentimes it twists the knife when you have a mesh component issue.

In this chapter, we are going to dig deeper on each smell using a simplified version of the design smell template proposed by S. G. Ganesh, Tushar Sharma, and Girish Suryanarayana.[2]

Cyclic Dependencies

Description: A cyclic dependency happens when a component (namely, A) depends on another component (namely, B) to perform its duties, which in turn depends on it (i.e., A). The same behavior can be extended to classes, functions, methods, and interfaces. The number of dependencies within the code is referred to as *coupling*.

Rationale: If a cyclic dependency happens when the components involved need to be modified, used, tested, extended, or used together, this is generally not a wanted behavior. Common cause of this type of smell is an improper design of responsibilities. A more subtle underlying issue is when a reference to self (this in Java) is passed between different components creating such dependency. Last, but not least, more complex systems might be nonobvious to mentally organize in terms of dependencies, hence resulting in unneeded introduction of flaws.

Violated principles: Readability, reusability, extensibility, testability, and maintainability.

Also known as: Circular dependency.

Variants: Circular imports, cyclic hierarchy.

Detection strategy: The simple case presented in the description could be spotted by simply carefully reading the code. However, cycles of dependencies can span across several components before returning to the starting point, hence closing the loop. A better approach in this case is to take a look at the class diagram. Inspect it to see if it behaves like a directed acyclic graph (DAG). If not, fix the cycles.

Suggested refactoring: Bad design is oftentimes the mother of cyclic dependencies. So first things first

1. *Rethink your design*: The cyclic dependency might just be the result of violating the single responsibility principle (SRP) (explained in the following). Possibly, resolving the SRP violation will fix cyclic dependency as well.

---

[2]Ganesh, S. G., Sharma, T., & Suryanarayana, G. (2013). Towards a Principle-based Classification of Structural Design Smells. Journal of Object Technology, 12(2), 1-1.

2. Otherwise, if and only if the given modules are cohesive and short enough, a simple fix is to just **merge the dependent modules together**.

3. If merging is not possible without breaking other principles, consider defining and introducing **interfaces** to solve the issue.

■ **Definition**   The single responsibility principle states that every component should only have one goal. When a component attempts to perform more than a single logical function, this principle is broken. For example, if a function is attempting to perform both addition and removal of an object to/from a newly invented data structure, it does not follow the single responsibility principle and hence is considered unclean code.

The following snippets show an example of cyclic imports. However, remember that the concept applies to classes and functions as well.

First, a module A is defined as

```
# I am moduleA, nice to meet you
import moduleB

def print_val():
    print('I am just an example.')

def calling_moduleB():
    moduleB.module_functionality()
```

Second, a second module B is defined as

```
# I am moduleB, nice to meet you too
import moduleA

def module_functionality():
    print ('I am doing nothing at all.')
    moduleA.print_val()
```

Finally, a module C that uses cyclic code

```
# I am moduleC
import moduleA

def show_dependency():
    print ('Such an interesting dependency.')
    moduleA.calling_moduleB()
```

As from the preceding snippet, a cyclic dependency exists since module A relies on module B, which in turn relies on module A (import statements).

Feature Density

Description: This defect happens when a component implements more than a single functionality. Specifically, we refer to feature density when such components have a lot of dependencies that are not clearly structured. Those dependencies are such that the calling component performs some duties (i.e., logical functionalities) that should be performed by the callee. This might be the case, for example, of an object depending on multiple other objects to perform its duties. However, instead of having structured dependencies, it uses and builds on top of them eventually performing functions that should have been implemented by the dependencies.

Rationale: This smell breaks the single responsibility principle. Hence, it comes with all the inherited flaws. Given multiple—eventually independent—functionalities into the same component, it increases the chances of adding dependencies from many more other pieces of code as it gets extended further. Furthermore, changes to the affected component will impact all the dependent abstractions, hence impacting on maintainability.

Violated principles: Maintainability and single responsibility principle.

Also known as: Feature envy.[3,4]

Detection strategy: For manual code reviews, check that Single responsibility principle is ensured. Each class, method, or function should have a single logical goal to be achieved.

Suggested refactoring: The solution to this smell is simple—keep logic around a single responsibility and cut the fat out. Move out methods that clearly need to be elsewhere. If several methods need to be factored out, it might be the case of having them in their own little class.

Let's build a fairly smart coffee machine to demonstrate feature density in the following snippet:

```python
# This is a very smart virtual coffee machine
class CoffeeMachine:

    def __init__(self, user):
        self.user = user
```

---

[3]D'Ambros, M., Bacchelli, A., & Lanza, M. (2010, July). On the impact of design flaws on software defects. In Quality Software (QSIC), 2010 10th International Conference on (pp. 23–31). IEEE.

[4]W. Li and R. Shatnawi, An Empirical Study of the Bad Smells and Class Error Probability in the Post-Release Object-Oriented System Evolution, J. Syst. Softw., 80(7): pp. 1120–1128, 2007.

```
def make_coffee(self, user):
    self.gather_user_preferences()
    print ('Work in progress. Wait a minute, please.')
    ...

def gather_user_preferences(self):
    preferred = user._preferred
    milk = user._milk
    print ('I am learning the type of coffee you like')
```

As you can see from the code, too much is achieved into the same class: doing coffee, managing user's information, and—if it was not enough—customizing the coffee type based on learned preferences. This is enough to break the single responsibility principle. However, also pay particular attention to the *gather_user_preferences* method. The coffee machine should not access to user information and figure on its own what the preferences for the specific user are.

Unstable Dependency

Description: It happens if a component depends on a less stable one. This applies to any type of component (e.g., classes, methods), scenario (e.g., APIs, backend software), and type of defect in the code (e.g., design, technical debt, security).

Rationale: When a component depends on less stable ones, it will be easier to break the code.

Violated principles: Maintainability.

Detection strategy: Some tools and metrics are still under development or tuning. For example, a formula has been proposed to express to which degree a dependency can be considered unstable.[5] The main concern expressed by the referenced work is that a package with a small number of bad dependencies may not be a smell. Hence, they use thresholds to signal this type of smell. However, more tuning of these thresholds might be needed.

Suggested refactoring: This smell is not always easy to fix. However, especially for production-ready code, try to find a more stable version of libraries used.

■ **Note** As in security, the overall security of a system is as strong as its weakest link, so the stability of a system is dependent on the stability of its most unstable component.

---

[5]Arcan - Fontana, Francesca Arcelli, et al. "Arcan: A tool for architectural smells detection." 2017 IEEE International Conf. on Software Architecture Workshops, ICSA Workshops 2017, Gothenburg, Sweden, April 5–7, 2017.

Figure 4-1 visually shows a relationship between a stable component and unstable one. As an example, the stable component is a clean coded component (e.g., a class) that imports another component (e.g., another class) which suffers from feature density.

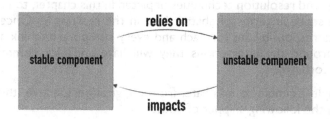

Figure 4-1. Unstable dependency

As a consequence, how clean the stable component really is depends on the feature dense one, resulting in a theoretically stable component which indirectly is as much stable as the unstable one.

Mashed Components

Description: As the opposite of the feature density defect, a mashed component is one that should logically be a single functionality, while scattered on different places on the code.

Rationale: Scattering code which should be logically in the same abstraction has similar impact on the number of dependencies like the feature density smell. Indeed, to obtain the overall wanted behavior, multiple components need to be involved into the computation process. This has a severe impact on all the major principles of well-designed software. Also known as scattered functionality smell, this can be defined—in other words—as multiple components that head to achieving the same high-level objective.

Violated principles: Readability, maintainability, reusability, and testability.

Also known as: Scattered functionality.[6,7]

Detection strategy: To detect this smell, take a look at diagrams (e.g., class diagrams) and inspect for highly coupled behavior. It might be the case of a mashed component smell.

---

[6]Tushar Sharma. (2017) [Designite-tools] (www.designite-tools.com/designite/does-your-architecture-smell/).

[7]Tushar Sharma. Does Your Architecture Smell? [Design Smells. Managing Technical Debt] (www.designsmells.com/articles/does-your-architecture-smell/).

Suggested refactoring: Rethink the provided abstractions and refactor the code accordingly. Remove any redundant code.

Finding the right trade-off between the two, hence having a well put together design, is not always obvious, and the only way to find it is, other than following the red flags and resolution techniques depicted in this chapter, to really think what make sense in terms of abstractions in the real world. Once you can clearly state responsibilities for each and every component, think about the problems around the interactions they will have and pick communication patterns accordingly.

A very simple example to illustrate, from a logical perspective, this smell is provided in the following snippet of code:

```python
# UserManager - 1
class FirstUserManager:

    def __init__(self, name, surname):
        self._name = name
        self._surname = surname
        self._printer = SecondUserManager()

    def print_user(self),
        self._printer.printing(self._name, self._surname)

# UserManager - 2
class SecondUserManager:

    def printing(self, name, surname):
        print ('Yeah, I just printing on screen.')
        ...
```

Basic functionalities that could be part of a single component are scattered across more than one functionality. A simple refactoring in this case would be to allow *FirstUserManager* to print user information on its own.

■ **Note** The example is provided for demonstration purposes. More complex duties like saving (e.g., database or file) or more complex logging should be in separate components.

Ambiguous Interfaces

Description: APIs should be extensible and flexible, not unclear or ambiguous. Ambiguity, as will be described in the following, can happen for several reasons.

Rationale: A fairly common example of an ambiguous interface[8] is when a component offers from a single entry point. This is, for example, the case where a class provides a single public method that allows for actually accessing the class behavior. In real-world scenario, it is like imagining a website that needs to offer login, logout, and password retrieval functionality, and all these features are modeled with a single general interface. When this smell arises, a review of the actual code is needed in order to have an understanding of what the affected interface is meant for. Another common case of ambiguity is when multiple (i.e., more than one) signatures are too similar (e.g., same method name but with slightly different parameters). What can happen is that under certain scenarios, both of them might be applied, causing ambiguity in which one should be used.

Violated principles: Readability, maintainability, and reusability.

Detection strategy: Scan the code to figure out where interactions between components in the system are not clearly modeled.

Suggested refactoring: Rethink the provided interfaces and refactor the code accordingly. Disclaimer: the sooner the properly designed interfaces, the better. Neglecting to properly design interfaces might cause integration issues later on when this smell is found and changes are needed.

Let's analyze a simple example of ambiguous interfaces:

```
# This is an example containing ambiguous interfaces
class Ambiguous:

    def ambiguity(name:object, surname: str):
        pass

    @overload
    def ambiguity(name:str, surname: object):
        pass
```

Consider the obvious case in which both name and surname are strings. In such conditions, both methods would apply.

In contrast, let's consider the following variation:

```
# This is an example containing ambiguous interfaces
class Ambiguous:

    def ambiguity(name:object, surname: object):
        pass
```

---

[8]J. Garcia, D. Popescu, G. Edwards, N. Medvidovic (2009), "Toward a Catalogue of Architectural Bad Smells". QoSA, pp. 146-162.

```
@overload
def ambiguity(name:str, surname: str):
    pass
```

As you can see, this code is cleaner, than the previous one due to the specificity of the signatures. Everything that is not of type (str, str) will be mapped to the first method with input type (object, object).

Mesh Components

Description: This is the case where components, are heavily coupled, with a lot of dependencies and oftentimes without clear and well-defined patterns.

Rationale: This smell might be caused by the mashed components smell; however, it is not always the case. It is a more general smell and the root cause might simply be a lack of abstraction and design patterns.

Violated principles: Maintainability, testability, readability, and reusability.

Also known as: Dense structure.

Detection strategy: Similar to the mashed components, to detect this smell, take a look at diagrams (e.g., class diagrams) and inspect for highly coupled behavior.

Suggested refactoring: As almost all the design issues, rethink the provided abstractions and refactor the code accordingly as necessary.

A simple example of this smell is shown in Figure 4-2.

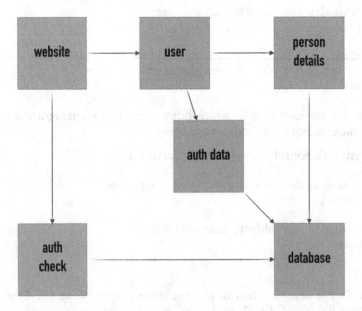

Figure 4-2. Mesh components

As you can see from the example, there is no clear structure on how the components interact with each other. Some simple fixes (i.e., adding patterns and structure) include adding an authentication manager as well as a more structured way to interact with the database (e.g., a database manager).

The example shown above is fairly simple and presents only single direction dependencies. However, scenarios in industrial code can definitely be more complex and convoluted than this one.

What happens to the previous example if also another dependency is present from person details to the user?

For example, the user has personal details modeled separately (hence the dependency from user to person details), but the person details class also interacts with the user to access to authentication data (dependency from person details to user).

This last scenario is not only an indicator of lack of proper abstractions but also introduces, because of it, more smelly code, in this case a cyclic dependency.

First Lady Components

Description: This kind of component will do all the possible work by itself. It reaches such a growth that it becomes really expensive to maintain. The first lady component puts the feature density smell to its extreme. However, while a feature dense component only attempts to build functionalities that are not part of its duties and still relying partially on other components, a first lady simply does not have dependencies to components that should abstract separate behavior. It simply implements them all.

Rationale: This type of components is a conglomerate of independent behavior. It is similar to the feature density smell, but it is exponential in the lack of abstraction and of the negative impacts it has. As an immediate consequence of implementing multiple independent behaviors, the design of components that depend on a single logical functionality implemented by the first lady also becomes unclean, cascading to a heavily coupled overall design. Indeed, a single lady introduces possibly unneeded dependencies and well as a single point of failure.

Violated principles: Readability, maintainability, reusability, single responsibility principle, and testability.

Also known as: God component.[9,10]

---

[9]Tushar Sharma. (2017) [Designite-tools] (www.designite-tools.com/designite/does-your-architecture-smell/).

[10]Tushar Sharma. Does Your Architecture Smell? [Design Smells. Managing Technical Debt] (www.designsmells.com/articles/does-your-architecture-smell/).

Detection strategy: Easily detect and inspect classes, modules, and functions. Those with a big number of lines of code (LOC) might be good candidates for this type of smell. It is also as simple as reading package name, class name, and the methods implemented in such a class. Simply reading them helps in spotting any behavior that does not belong to the given abstraction.

Suggested refactoring: Oftentimes this smell happens due to a lack of abstraction. Once you detect the affected components, rethinking the problem and properly defining behavior help in removing flaws.

A simple example of single lady is the scenario where there is a class that models the behavior of a user. This class, however, also implements general logging capabilities within the system. As an immediate effect, every other component that needs logging capability will have to depend on the user abstraction to access to logging.

As a cascading issue, what can also happen is that a developer reading the code can quickly, by reading packages and class names, assume that the system does not provide logging capabilities, hence providing an alternative implementation of logging. This not only ends in very unclean code, but it causes also time to be wasted to potentially reinvent the wheel.

That's Not My Responsibility Component or Bossy Component

Description: At the opposite end of the first lady, this component likes to delegate stuff that it doesn't want to deal with to other components. This component is not nice to have in code and oftentimes it twists the knife in the mesh components issue.

Rationale: This component also breaks the single responsibility principle—single means one, not none. Hence, it inherits all the flaws of mashed component smell, multiplied by ten.

Violated principles: Readability, maintainability, reusability, and testability.

Detection strategy: Inspect heavily coupled components. Is the caller only delegating logic to other components?

Suggested refactoring: Rethink the functionalities and refactor accordingly. Check if this abstraction is really needed.

The following code demonstrates a bossy component:

```python
# I am the boss
class BossyComponent:

    def do(self):
        Mario.check_architecture()
        Lisa.check_code()
        Luigi.test()
        self.something_left_for_me()

    def something_left_for_me(self):
        print ('I am the boss, I am doing nothing. Hee Hee. ')

class Mario:
    @staticmethod
    def check_architecture():
        print ('Ok')

class Lisa:
    @staticmethod
    def check_code():
        print ('Ok')

class Luigi:
    @staticmethod
    def test():
        print ('Ok')
```

The code is self-explanatory. You might just be curious why I used static methods. Well, it looks more authoritative, isn't it?

The core issue of this smell is not that it has dependencies per se: we reuse behavior from other components when needed. Otherwise, no code in the world would be clean or even written. Instead, the key issue is when we introduce an abstraction that simply gathers together dependencies without adding value on its own.

At the end of the day, detecting and fixing this smell is really about asking yourself if the abstraction is really needed and has a purpose (no more than one, but a single one).

■ **Note** I like to refer to this component as the bossy component as well. The rest of the book will use both names interchangeably.

Summary

Even great clean code will start to smell over time. As you add functionalities and complexities, and as the programmers work on the code changes, the defects will build up and the smell will start to develop. That's normal and that's why healthy code requires incremental improvements and reviews to stay that way.

It is like going to the gym. You work hard and finally achieve the glorious six pack abs you've dreamed about. You are the happiest person on earth. How long do you think that happiness will last if you suddenly stop training and watching what you eat? Your dream abs will go away in no time.

So please, smell your code and do it often.

In the next chapter, we will introduce how to have a more comprehensive view at the overall structure of the code by means of looking at software architectures.

Further Reading

Smelling the code is for sure not a brand new topic, while often neglected. If you have to pick just one other book to read on the topic, go for Martin Fowler's *Patterns of Enterprise Application Architecture*—an always current reference for design wisdom. Another good source for design smells is *Refactoring for Software Design Smells: Managing Technical Debt* by Girish Ganesh Samarthyam and Tushar Sharma.

Code Review Checklist

1. Are *cyclic dependencies* present in the code?

2. Is the code *feature dense*? More than one feature per component is enough to have this smell.

3. Are the dependencies stable?

4. Does the code have *mashed components*?

5. Are APIs clearly defined?

6. Are *mesh components* present?

7. Are *first lady components* present?

8. Are *bossy components* present?

9. Does the class diagram behave like a DAG?

10. Does each and every class, method, or function have a single logical responsibility to be achieved?

11. Does the class diagram show highly coupled components?

12. Is there any function, method, or class with a big LOC number?

Software Architectures

There is nothing new under the sun. It has all been done before.

—Sherlock Holmes in Sir Arthur Conan Doyle's
"A Study in Scarlet" (1887)

In Chapter 2, we started taking a look at some of the possible dos and don'ts around the design phase and introduced why software architectures are important. However, this aspect requires a deeper look. In particular, a strong emphasis on using design patterns properly is needed when dealing with architectures.

Hence, in this chapter, we will dive into the following aspects:

- Design patterns
- What each pattern does, how they are used, when to use them, and what not to do
- Main issues at design time

© Giuliana Carullo 2020
G. Carullo, *Implementing Effective Code Reviews*,
https://doi.org/10.1007/978-1-4842-6162-0_5

Code Under the Shower

If the architecture smells, a shower is needed to rinse out the obvious dirty issues so we can better scrub out the worse ones. One of the common ways to improve the design is by using appropriate design patterns to minimize the dirt. Design patterns can be broken down into four main categories:

- *Creational*: Which deals with common pattern for object creation

- *Structural*: Which aims at simplifying the relations between components

- *Behavioral*: Which establishes common pattern for communications

- *Concurrency*: Which is designed to address multithreading scenarios

In this section, we will address the main patterns in the first three categories as shown in Table 5-1. Concurrency patterns will not be considered in this book. Although very interesting and useful, they are intentionally left out of its scope. What this book is meant to provide, indeed, is a well-rounded review yet not dealing with all the intricacies of definitely more complex scenarios. However, foundations about concurrent programming will be discussed in Chapter 9, to provide some general guidance in the area.

Table 5-1. Design Patterns

Class	Patterns
Creational	Singleton
	Lazy initialization
	Builder
	Abstract factory
	Factory method
Structural	Adapter
	Decorator
	Façade
	Composite
Behavioral	Publisher-subscriber
	Iterator
	Visitor
	State
	Chain of responsibility
Concurrency	See Chapter 9

■ **Note** The images accompanying the pattern descriptions aim to illustrate the general concepts. They are not meant to model the relative Python structure.

Creational Design Patterns: The Days of Creation

In this section, we will explore some of the main *creational* design patterns (Table 5-2).

Table 5-2. Creational Design Pattern

Class	Patterns
Creational	Singleton
	Lazy initialization
	Builder
	Abstract factory
	Factory method

Singleton

A *singleton* is probably the easiest pattern you can encounter. It aims at restricting the number of instances of a class.

How

This pattern hides the constructor of the class by means of declaring it *private*. A get_instance() method is used to create the instance upon the first call and returning the unique instance at later invocations. See Figure 5-1.

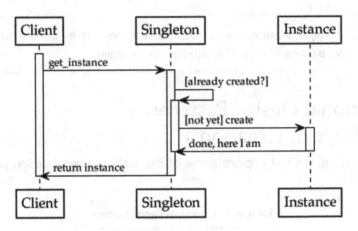

Figure 5-1. Singleton. Getting some "me" time

When

A singleton might be required when

- There is a need to implement controls to access to shared resources (e.g., in the context of concurrency).

- A single resource is accessed from several parts of the system.

- Only a single instance of a class is needed.

A common scenario is to use a singleton for logging purposes.

A very simple implementation of the singleton is in the following snippet of code:

```python
class Singleton:

    def __init__(self):
        if Singleton.__instance:
            raise Exception("I am a singleton!")
        else:
            Singleton.__instance = self

    @staticmethod
    def get_instance():
        if not Singleton.__instance:
            Singleton()
        return Singleton.__instance
```

Guideline

Singleton inspires controversial thoughts. Some people love it; some do not. Someone else both hates it and loves it at the same time. From time to time, the singleton has been pointed out as a *"bad smell."* One of the reasons is that it can easily fall into the *first lady* category analyzed in Chapter 4. You might have this big giant global instance trying to do everything. Personally, I do not see a problem in the singleton per se. If something similar happens, you are just using the wrong pattern for the problem you are trying to solve.

Lazy Initialization

This pattern allows to instantiate an object only when actually required.

How

Implementing this pattern is a simple task. Instead of creating the object into the constructor, it is created upon the first actual request that needs to be performed on the instance. See Figure 5-2.

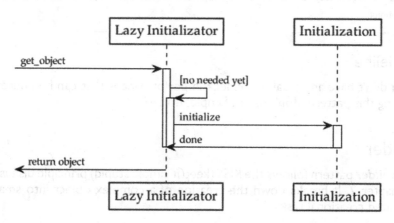

Figure 5-2. Lazy initialization. From time to time, procrastinating is done for a good cause

The following is a snippet of code showing an example of lazy initialization:

```
class MyHeavyObject:
    def __init__(self):
        self._heavy = []
```

```
@property
def heavy(self):
    if not self._heavy:
        print ('I am doing heavy computation.')
        # expensive computation
        ...
```

When

Lazy instantiations are used when the heavy lifting computational job the object needs to do can be postponed for performance reasons. A common example of implementation is its alternative lazy load. A *lazy load* is used when integration is needed with a database (DB). Data from the DB is loaded in memory only when required.

This pattern is more on the performance side of the house rather than just clean code. There is no strict rule on when it can be used.

■ **Note** I've referred to the lazy load as a common implementation for reading data from a database. However, lazy initialization can be applied to a multitude of applications including web applications.

Guideline

If you don't have an actual bottleneck in performances that can be improved by using this pattern, don't use it. Simple, isn't it?

Builder

The **builder** pattern follows the *KISS* (keep it simple stupid) principle discussed in Chapter 2. It breaks down the creation of a complex object into smaller separated creational tasks.

How

The **builder** exposes the interface to create the complex object as a single task. However, it internally manages the calls to the **concrete builders** each performing one step of the entire processing needed. See Figure 5-3.

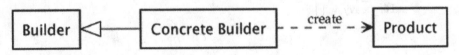

Figure 5-3. Builder. Keep it simple

A simplified version of the builder pattern in Python code is shown in the following:

```python
# Abstract Builder
class Builder(object):

    def __init__(self):
        self.laptop = None

    def new_laptop(self):
        self.laptop = Laptop()

# Concrete Builder
class BuilderVirtualLaptop(Builder):

    def build_cpu(self):
        self.laptop.cpu ='whatever cpu'

    def build_ram(self):
        self.laptop.ram = 'whatever ram'
    ...

# Product
class Laptop(object):

    def __init__(self):
        self.cpu = None
        self.ram = None
        ...

    # print of laptop info
    def __repr__(self):
        return 'Laptop with cpu = {} and ram = {}'.format(self.cpu, self.ram)

# Director
class Director(object):

    def __init__(self):
        self.builder = BuilderVirtualLaptop()

    def construct_laptop(self):
        self.builder.new_laptop()
        self.builder.build_cpu()
        self.builder.build_ram()
        ...

    def get_building(self):
        return self.builder.laptop
```

```
#Simple Client
if __name__ =="__main__":
    director = Director()
    director.construct_laptop()
    building = director.get_building()
    print (building)
```

The example code shows the creation of a laptop. Virtually, a laptop can be broken down into several creational tasks that need to be performed in order to have the final product such as CPU, RAM, disk, and so on.

When

In general, this pattern is helpful when the final object can be constructed via an arbitrary (depending on the context) number of tasks. The builder can be considered when the solutions can benefit from

1. Better control of the creational process.

2. Hiding complex creation with the builder allows for easier to read and use objects.

3. If any of the creational steps need to change, this will only affect a limited portion of the code (i.e., the builder itself)—not directly impacting the code that builds on top of the created object.

Guideline

The definition is fairly simple; thus, stick with it, taking into account that embracing this design pattern has minor disadvantages including writing more lines of code (LOCs). A signal that a builder is not appropriate, or not appropriately used, is when the builder constructor has a long list of parameters required to deal with each concrete builder.

Consider, for example, the case where you have a pub and you offer to customers the option to customize their hamburger meal with several toppings.

Building such hamburger might have a long list of toppings (cheese, bacon, lettuce, tomato, onion, ketchup, etc.)

As the business needs to offer a broader choice of toppings to customers, the initially simple builder

```
Hamburger(cheese)
```

can quickly escalate to

```
Hamburger(cheese, lettuce, tomato, onion, bacon, you_name_it)
```

In such case, proper use of the builder would entail the possibility of customizing the order by, for example, set functions instead of providing support for each and every topping at creation time.

■ **Note**   When using this pattern, do not neglect to think longer term. Back to our burger example. What if you are offering only two options, hamburger and cheeseburger, but you ideally will add also customization with toppings in the future? Looking a bit ahead of times can help in achieving the right design and usage from the start.

Abstract Factory

The **abstract factory** allows you to hide complexity during object creation. This pattern enables to create different versions of the same object.

How

The abstract factory component creates the actual object. It internally manages different components that represent different flavors of the final product. See Figure 5-4.

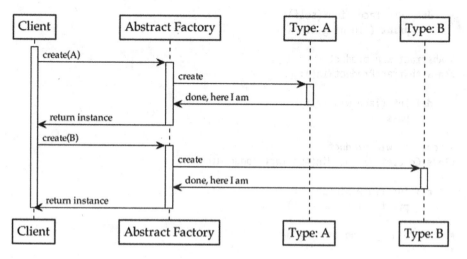

Figure 5-4. Abstract factory. Simple is better than complex

An example of Python implementation is in the following:

```python
# Interface for operations supported by the factory
class AbstractFactory():

    def create_linux(self):
        pass

    def create_win(self):
        pass

# Concrete factory. Managing object creation.
class ConcreteFactoryOS(AbstractFactory):

    def create_linux(self):
        return ConcreteProductLinux()

    def create_win(self):
        return ConcreteProductWin()

# Abstract Linux product
class AbstractProductLinux():

    def interface_linux(self):
        pass

# Concrete linux product
class ConcreteProductLinux(AbstractProductLinux):

    def interface_linux(self):
        print ('running linux')

# Abstract win product
class AbstractProductWin():

    def interface_win(self):
        pass

# Concrete win product
class ConcreteProductWin(AbstractProductWin):

    def interface_win(self):
        print ('running win')

# Factory usage and testing out
if __name__ == "__main__":
    factory = ConcreteFactoryOS()
    product_linux = factory.create_linux()
```

```
product_win = factory.create_win()
product_linux.interface_linux()
product_win.interface_win()
```

When

In the example code, we have our laptop, but no operating system (OS) is on top yet. The OS can be modeled as an *abstract factory*, and it returns an instance of one of the different flavors (different components) it supports (e.g., Linux, Mac, Windows). In general, this pattern can be used every time we support different variations of the same object.

Guideline

This pattern is a nice way to hide complexity when the *caller* does not need to deal with underlying computation. Common sense, do not add complexity when not required. Indeed, adding a new product is not that scalable since it requires new implementations for each factory.

Factory Method

The factory method is similar to the abstract factory, thus often confused. Guess what? Instead of building a *factory* object, this pattern can be synthesized as a *factory* (actual) method.

How

By means of inheritance, the factory method can be overwritten to implement different flavors. See Figure 5-5.

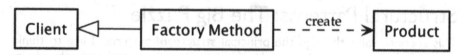

Figure 5-5. Factory method. Complex is better than complicated

An example of Python implementation is in the following:

```python
# First Product
class ProductA(object):

    def __init__(self):
        print ('Building Product A')
```

```
# Second Product
class ProductB(object):

    def __init__(self):
        print ('Building Product B')

# Factory Method
def factory_method(product_type):
    if product_type == 'PA':
        return ProductA()
    elif product_type == 'PB':
        return ProductB()
    else:
        raise ValueError('Cannot find: {}'.format(product_type))

# Client: testing out
if __name__ == '__main__':
    for product_type in ('PA', 'PB'):
        product = factory_method(product_type)
        print(str(product))
```

When

In general, instead of dealing with the composition of different sub-objects, this pattern is meant to create an object hiding internal details, while being a single concrete product. This is opposite to the abstract factory.

Guideline

The recommendation is exactly the same as the abstract factory. Do not opt for factories when object abstraction is not needed.

Structural Patterns: The Big Puzzle

This section walks through the principal *structural* patterns. I like to think about this category as a big puzzle. You have interfaces and code already in place, but you still have to make all the components interact and work in the best possible way. The following patterns help in achieving it. See Table 5-3.

Table 5-3. Structural Design Pattern

Class	Patterns
Structural	Adapter
	Decorator
	Façade
	Composite

Adapter

The adapter is also known as **wrapper**. It wraps another object, redefining its interface.

How

A new class simply encapsulated the incompatible object, thus providing the desired interface. See Figure 5-6.

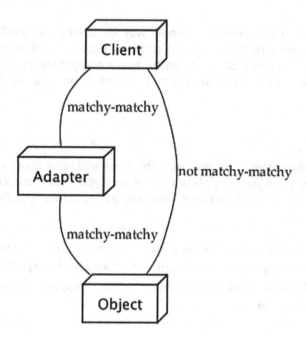

Figure 5-6. Adapter. A piece of the puzzle

The following code shows a general implementation of this pattern:

```python
# Adapter: our wrapping class
class Adapter:

    def __init__(self):
        self._adaptee = Adaptee()

    def request(self):
        self._adaptee.legacy_request()

# Adaptee: existing interface
class Adaptee:

    def legacy_request(self):
        print ('Matchy-matchy now! yay!')

# Client: testing out
if __name__ == "__main__":
    adapter = Adapter()
    adapter.request()
```

When

The adapter pattern provides a simple way for solving compatibility issues between different interfaces. Suppose a *caller* is expecting a different interface from a certain object (*callee*), it can be made compatible by means of the *adapter*. They can be handy for legacy software. It enables reusability for a lower price.

Guideline

Likewise, all the patterns we discuss in this book add complexity to the code. Always follow the KISS principle and make sure you have interface problems between various components when deciding to implement an adapter.

■ **Note** As for the builder pattern, do not neglect to think longer term. Do you foresee possible changes to an interface you are designing? Adding an adapter might be very well appropriate. At the same time, if an interface can flexibly be changed without causing dependencies to break, the adapter would add unneeded complexity.

Decorator

The decorator enables reusability by means of enhancing an object behavior.

How

Similar to the adapter pattern, it wraps the object adding the wanted functionalities. See Figure 5-7.

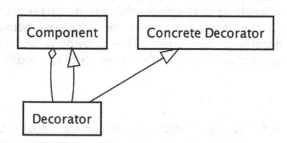

Figure 5-7. Decorator. Some software craft

A simplified example of decorator is shown in the following snippet of code:

```python
# Decorator interface
class Decorator:

    def __init__(self, component):
        self._component = component

    def operation(self):
        pass

# Decorator
class ConcreteDecorator(Decorator):
    """
    Add responsibilities to the component.
    """

    def operation(self):
        self._component.operation()
        print ('And some more makeup!)'

# Component that needs to be decorated
class Component:

    def operation(self):
        print ('I have some makeup on!)'
```

```
# Client: testing out
if __name__ == "__main__":
    component = Component()
    decorator = ConcreteDecorator(component)
    decorator.operation()
```

When

The decorator design pattern helps in fighting the first lady component smell. Thus, it adds functionalities to an object, while maintaining single responsibility principle. Indeed, the decorator allows for additional behavior without impacting the decorated component. They provide a nice alternative to inheritance and are useful when the behavior needs to be modified at runtime.

Guideline

Simple yet powerful. But, don't make the decorator become the new first lady. Decorators can complicate the initialization process and the overall design (depending on how many decorators you implement). Make sure to not overcomplicate the design (special attention to multiple layers of decorators): you might be pushing decorators beyond the purpose they are meant to serve.

Facade

A facade can be somehow ideally associated with the abstract factory. However, instead of creating an object, it provides a simpler interface for other more complex interfaces.

How

This pattern provides a brand new higher-level interface in order to make the subsystems (often independent classes with complex logic) easier to use and interact with. See Figure 5-8.

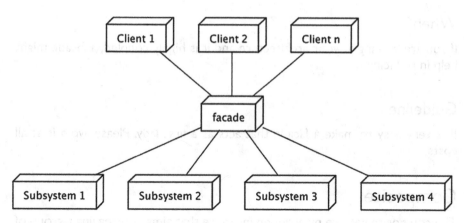

Figure 5-8. Facade. Putting it all together

A simplified example of a facade is shown in the following snippet of code:

```
# Facade
class Facade:

    def __init__(self):
        self._subsystem_1 = Subsystem1()
        self._subsystem_2 = Subsystem2()

    def operation(self):
        self._subsystem_1.operation1()
        self._subsystem_2.operation2()

# Subsystem
class Subsystem1:

    def operation1(self):
        print ('Subsystem 1: complex operations')

# Subsystem
class Subsystem2:

    def operation2(self):
        print ('Subsystem 2: complex operations')

# Client
if __name__ == "__main__":
    facade = Facade()
    facade.operation()
```

When

If you are looking at your architecture and it is highly coupled, a facade might help in reducing it.

Guideline

It is very easy to make a facade that acts as a first lady. Please avoid it at all costs.

Composite

The composite pattern provides an interface that aims at managing a group of complex objects and single objects exposing similar functionalities in a uniform manner.

How

It composes objects into a tree structure, in such a way that nodes in the tree—regardless of whether they are a leaf (single object) or complex object (i.e., non-leaves)—can be accessed in a similar way, abstracting complexity to the *caller*. In particular, when a method is called on a node, if it is a leaf, the node manages it autonomously. Otherwise, the node calls the method upon its children. See Figure 5-9.

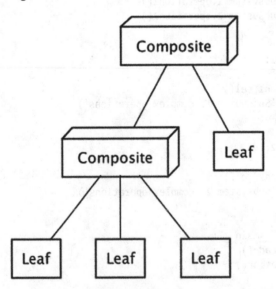

Figure 5-9. Composite. Uniform is good

An example of a composite pattern is shown in the following snippet of code:

```python
# Abstract Class
# Defining the interface for all the components in the composite
class Component():

    def operation(self):
        pass

# Composite: managing the tree structure
class Composite(Component):
    def __init__(self):
        self._children = set()

    def operation(self):
        print ('I am a Composite!')
        for child in self._children:
            child.operation()

    def add(self, component):
        self._children.add(component)

    def remove(self, component):
        self._children.discard(component)

# Leaf node
class Leaf(Component):

    def operation(self):
        print ('I am a leaf!')

# Client: testing out
if __name__ == "__main__":
    # Tree structure
    leaf = Leaf()
    composite = Composite()
    composite.add(leaf)
    composite_root = Composite()
    leaf_another = Leaf()
    composite_root.add(composite)
    composite_root.add(leaf_another)

    # Same operation on the entire tree
    composite_root.operation()
```

When

This pattern can be used when you have to selectively manage a group of heterogeneous and hierarchical objects as they would ideally be the same object. Indeed, this pattern allows for same exploration of the hierarchy, independently from the node type (i.e., leaf and composite).

As a concrete example, think about the hierarchical structure of folders, subfolders, and files on a computer. And consider that the only operation allowed is deletion. For every folder, subfolder, or file, you want the delete operation to be uniformly applied to any substructure (if any). In other words, if you delete a folder, you want to delete also all the subfolders and files contained in it. Modeling this structure as a composite would allow you to perform the deletion in a simpler and cleaner manner.

Guideline

Take a deeper look at your tree structure. A lot of initialized while not used nodes at the frontier (i.e., leaves) might signal that some refactoring is required.

Behavioral Design Patterns: Behave Code, Behave!

Finally, this section explores *behavioral* patterns: they help in designing common relationships between components. See Table 5-4.

Table 5-4. Behavioral Design Pattern

Class	Patterns
Behavioral	Observer
	Publisher-subscriber
	Iterator
	Visitor
	State
	Chain of responsibility

Observer

In operating systems, a common way of notifying changes happening in the system is the **polling** and **interrupts** mechanisms. In the context of higher-level programming, a smarter way for notifying changes has been ideated: the **observer** pattern.

How

A component, namely, a *subject*, whose state needs to be notified stores a list of dependencies, namely, *observers*. Each and every time a change occurs in the subject, it notifies it to its stored list of observers as shown in Figure 5-10.

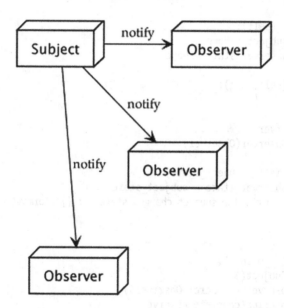

Figure 5-10. Observer. At a glance

An example of an observer pattern is shown in the following snippet of code:

```python
# The observable subject
class Subject:

    def __init__(self):
        self._observers = set()
        self._state = None

    def subscribe(self, observer):
        observer._subject = self
        self._observers.add(observer)
```

```python
    def unsubscribe(self, observer):
        observer._subject = None
        self._observers.discard(observer)

    def _notify(self):
        for observer in self._observers:
            observer.update(self._state)

    def set_state(self, arg):
        self._state = arg
        self._notify()

# Interface for the Observer
class Observer():

    def __init__(self):
        self._subject = None
        self._observer_state = None

    def update(self, arg):
        pass

# Concrete observer
class ConcreteObserver(Observer):

    def update(self, subject_state):
        self._observer_state = subject_state
        print ('Uh oh! The subject changed state to: {}'.format(subject_state))
        # ...

# Testing out
if __name__ == "__main__":
    subject = Subject()
    concrete_observer = ConcreteObserver()
    subject.subscribe(concrete_observer)

    # External changes: testing purposes
    subject.set_state('Ping')
    subject.set_state('Pong')
```

Note The ordering of notifications with this pattern is not strictly related to the ordering of registration.

When

The observer pattern can be used when you need different objects to perform—automatically—some functions based on the state of another one (one to many). It generally suits well cases where broadcasting of information needs to happen and the subject does not need to know specifics or the number of observers.

Guideline

Once again, keep it simple and do not add unnecessary complexity. Always carefully consider the context: do you have observers that might not be interested to all the status changes? This pattern may notify observers also of changes that they are not interested in.

Publisher-Subscriber

Similar to observer patterns, publisher-subscriber patterns enable you to monitor state changes.

How

As confusing as it might initially sound, this pattern is very similar to observer patterns, but they are not actually the same. There are two basic components: **publisher**, the entity whose state is monitored, and **subscriber**, the one that is interested in receiving state changes.

The main difference is that the dependency between them is abstracted by a third component—often referred to as **broker**—that manages the state's update as shown in Figure 5-11. As a consequence, different from the observer, publisher and subscribers do not know about each other.

■ **Note**   A common way for brokers to identify which message needs to be sent to whom is by means of topics. A topic is nothing else than an expression of interest in a specific category of message to be received. Think about subscribing to a mailing list of a library, but you only want to receive messages only for programming and fantasy books. Programming and fantasy would be the topics you subscribed to.

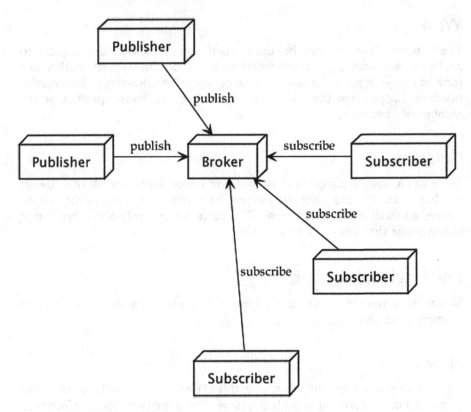

Figure 5-11. Publisher-subscriber. Please, let me know what's going on

An example of a publisher-subscriber pattern is shown in the following snippet of code:

```
# Publisher
class Publisher:

    def __init__(self, broker):
        self.state = None
        self._broker = broker

    def set_state(self, arg):
        self._state = arg
        self._broker.publish(arg)

# Subscriber
class Subscriber():

    def __init__(self):
        self._publisher_state = None
```

```python
    def update(self, state):
        self._publisher_state = state
        print ('Uh oh! The subject changed state to: {}'.format(state))
        # ...

# Broker
class Broker():

    def __init__(self):
        self._subscribers = set()
        self._publishers = set()

        # Setting up a publisher for testing purposes
        pub = Publisher(self)
        self._publishers.add(pub)

    # Triggering changes: testing purposes
    def trigger(self):
        for pub in self._publishers:
            pub.set_state('Ping')

    def subscribe(self, subscriber):
        self._subscribers.add(subscriber)

    def unsubscribe(self, subscriber):
        self._subscribers.discard(subscriber)

    def publish(self, state):
        for sub in self._subscribers:
            sub.update(state)

# Testing out
if __name__ == "__main__":
    # Setting an example
    broker = Broker()
    subscriber = Subscriber()
    broker.subscribe(subscriber)

    # External changes: testing purposes
    broker.trigger()
```

> ■ **Note**   Be aware that the preceding code is only for showcasing the interactions between the two main components. Some methods—for example, trigger()—are added only to allow a simple flow of execution.

When

This third-party exchange is helpful in any context where message exchange is required without components (publisher with relative subscribers) being aware of each other's existence. It is common to find pub-sub applications in almost any distributed message exchanging scenarios. For example, in the Internet of Things (IoT) world, tools such as Mosquitto and MQTT[1] are commonly used to implement publisher-subscriber that allows for message exchanges between distributed elements in the network.

■ **Note**   As you can imagine from the IoT example, any application of this pattern can use, but it is not limited to, a single publisher. Indeed, this pattern can be generalized to allow exchange of messages between any arbitrary number of publishers and subscribers.

Guideline

Do not overlook the scalability requirements of your solution. The broker might constitute a bottleneck for the entire message exchange.

Iterator

The iterator allows to navigate elements within an object, abstracting internal management.

How

Commonly, this pattern exposes two methods *next()* and *hasNext()* to perform the traversal. See Figure 5-12. Python implementations normally require an iterable object to implement:

1. *Iter*: Which returns the instance object

2. *Next*: Which will return the next value of the *iterable*

---

[1]https://mosquitto.org/

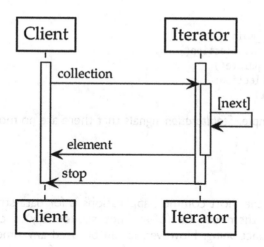

Figure 5-12. Iterator. Looking forward

A simple implementation of these two methods is presented in the following snippet:

```python
# Our collection of elements
class MyCollection():

    def __init__(self):
        self._data = list()

    def populate(self):
        for el in range(0, 10):
            self._data.append(el)

    def __iter__(self):
        return Iterator(self._data)

# Our iterator
class Iterator():

    def __init__(self, data):
        self._data = data
        self._counter = 0

    def next(self):
        if self._counter == len(self._data):
            raise StopIteration
        to_ret = self._data[self._counter]
        self._counter = self._counter + 1
        return to_ret
```

```
# Testing out
if __name__ == "__main__":
    collection = MyCollection()
    collection.populate()
    for el in collection:
        print (el)
```

In the code example, *StopIteration* signals that there are no more elements in the collection.

When

Probably one of the most common applications is for data structures where elements within them can be (oftentimes sequentially) accessed without knowing inner functioning. However, it can be used any time a traversal is needed without introducing changes to current interfaces.

Guideline

If the collection is small and simple, it might be not really required.

Visitor

The visitor allows you to decouple operational logic (i.e., algorithms) that would be—otherwise—scattered throughout different similar objects.

How

A **visitor** provides a *visit()* interface that allows to traverse the objects. A **ConcreteVisitor** implements the actual traversal. A **visitable** interface defines an *accept()* method. A **ConcreteVisitable** given the visitor object implements the accept operation. See Figure 5-13.

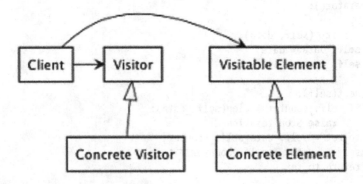

Figure 5-13. Visitor. I'll be there in a second

An example of a visitor pattern is shown in the following snippet of code:

```python
# Visitable supported operations
class VisitableElement():

    def accept(self, visitor):
        pass

# Concrete element to be visited
class ConcreteElement(VisitableElement):

    def __init__(self):
        self._el = 'Concrete element'

    def accept(self, visitor):
        visitor.visit(self)

# Visitor allowed operations
class Visitor():

    def visit(self, concrete_element_a):
        pass

# Implementing actual visit
class ConcreteVisitor(Visitor):

    def visit(self, concrete_element):
        print ('Visiting {}'.format(concrete_element._el))

# Testing out
if __name__ == "__main__":
    concrete_visitor = ConcreteVisitor()
    concrete_element = ConcreteElement()
    concrete_element.accept(concrete_visitor)
```

When

An example of an application of the visitor pattern is within data structures for tree traversal (e.g., pre-order, in-order, post-order). It suites fairly well treelike structures (e.g., syntax parsing), but is not strictly tight to these cases. Visitor pattern is not used only for treelike structures. Generally speaking, it can be applied when a complex computation needs to be applied depending on the object traversed. Back to our folder example, folder deletion can be performed at every layer (subfolder, files), yet the actual deletion requires different code for the operation to be performed.

Guideline

Avoid building visitors around unstable components. If the hierarchy is likely to change over time, the visitor pattern may not be appropriate. If the structure is stable and you want to apply the same function within it, it is more likely that the visitor pattern might suit your needs.

State

The state pattern enables context-aware objects.

How

The state pattern design is fairly simple: a context that represents the external interface, a state abstract class, and different state implementations that define the actual states. See Figure 5-14.

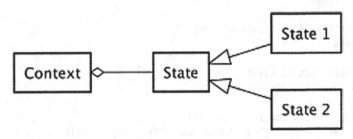

Figure 5-14. State. How are you doing?

The following is a simple implementation of the state design pattern:

```python
# Context definition
class Context:

    def __init__(self, state):
        self._state = state

    def manage(self):
        self._state.behave()

# Abstract State class
class State():

    def behave(self):
        pass
```

```
# Concrete State Implementation
class ConcreteState():

    def behave(self):
        print ('State specific behaviour!')

# Testing out
if __name__ == "__main__":
    state = ConcreteState()
    context = Context(state)
    context.manage()
```

When

The state pattern is helpful each time the behavior of an object is dependent of its state. In other words, it is applicable when the objects require changes in behavior depending on the state's changes.

The state pattern is commonly used in user interface (UI) development. React[2] provides a state built-in object that allows to dynamically reflect changes in state into the displayed UI.

Guideline

Pay close attention to when you actually use it. The number of states might exponentially grow, hence impacting the complexity of the code. It is also worth noticing that storing data that does not change in a state object is not considered a good practice due to its impact on readability: it does not necessarily affect performances, yet storing data elsewhere might increase how easy to use it would be.

Back to our react example: if the state does not change (e.g., all we want the user to see is a blank page with the title "Hello World!"), there is no real need to increase the complexity of the code for a page which is not dynamic.

Chain of Responsibility

The *chain of responsibility* pattern fosters decoupling between the sender of a request and the receiver.

---

[2]https://reactjs.org/

How

More objects within a pipeline are given a chance to handle an incoming request. In particular, the request is passed sequentially through the pipeline until an object is actually able to handle it. See Figure 5-15.

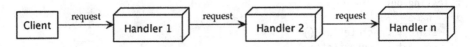

Figure 5-15. Chain of responsibility. Micromanaging is never the case

The following is a simple implementation of the chain of responsibility design pattern:

```python
# Handler Interface
class Handler():

    def __init__(self,request=None, successor=None):
        self._successor = successor

    def handle_request(self):
        pass

# Concrete Handler
class IntegerHandler(Handler):

    def handle_request(self):
        if request.get_type() is int:
            print (self.__class__.__name__)
        elif self._successor is not None:
            self._successor.handle_request()

# Another Concrete Handler
class StringHandler(Handler):

    def handle_request(self):
        if request.get_type() is str:
            print (self.__class__.__name__)
        elif self._successor is not None:
            self._successor.handle_request()

# Simple Request object
class Request():

    def __init__(self):
        self._el = 'I am a string'
```

```
    def get_type(self):
        return type(self._el)
# Testing out
if __name__ == "__main__":
    request = Request()
    string_handler = StringHandler(request=request)
    int_handler = IntegerHandler(request=request,successor=string_handler)
    int_handler.handle_request()
```

When

In cases when you want to abstract the processing pipeline by allowing a request to travel until it finds a handler able to take charge of it. It is a pretty handy pattern because you can decide which and in which order handlers are added to the chain.

Guideline

Back to nonfunctional requirements. Keep an eye on the required performances. Too many handlers (executed sequentially, in worst case skipping up to the very last handler in the chain) might impact code performances. Also bear in mind that debugging this pattern could be fairly difficult.

Summary

In this chapter, we provided guidance on the most common design patterns: how do they work, when to use them, and issues to consider for each of them.

Main takeaways

- Design patterns are meant to provide solutions for common problems. When choosing or reviewing design patterns in the codebase, consider if the problem you are trying to solve is very similar to the specific goal of the design pattern you want to use in your implementation.

- As always, keep it simple.

In the next chapter, we will go another step higher from the nitty-gritty details of code alone by providing guidelines from a design perspective.

Further Reading

Design patterns are widely used and discussed given their importance, ranging from basic design patterns explored in *Design Patterns: Elements of Reusable Object-Oriented Software* by Erich Gamma and colleagues (Addison-Wesley Professional, 1994) to more advanced enterprise patterns in *Patterns of Enterprise Application Architecture* by Martin Fowler (Addison-Wesley Professional, 2002). The latter is probably one of my absolutely preferred books on the topic; give it a try if you are serious about design patterns.

Code Review Checklist

1. Are you using design patterns properly?

2. Are the patterns the optimal choice based on requirements?

3. Are performances taken into account when choosing the design pattern you are inspecting?

4. Is the decorator a *first lady*?

5. Does the pattern hinder performance requirements?

6. Is your singleton behaving like a *first lady*?

From Scratch

You see, but you do not observe. The distinction is clear.

—Sherlock Holmes in Sir Arthur Conan Doyle's
"A Scandal in Bohemia" (1891)

Now that you know what to look for during a review, let's talk about what to do the moment you start reviewing the code, the architecture, and, equally important, the overall design and the understanding of the problem. Looking at the problem and its high-level requirements is important both before starting to write any code and during development time to ensure the code is scaling and growing in the direction it is meant to.

Hence, this chapter will explore some of the important collateral aspects to look at as regards the overall software design and its requirements.

Note If you are developing a software and you suddenly come to realize that the system is not performing or acting as expected, please, resist the urge of rewriting the entire code altogether. More likely than not, the work of many developers has been put into that code and not all of it is bad and not responding to an actual need. The only option for completely throwing away a fairly big portion of code and rewriting it in its entirety is if those developers who worked on it went 100% bananas and understood nothing, which is very, very unlikely to happen.

© Giuliana Carullo 2020
G. Carullo, *Implementing Effective Code Reviews*,
https://doi.org/10.1007/978-1-4842-6162-0_6

Problem Statement

Uh, Houston, we've had a problem.

—Jack Swigert, Apollo 13 Technical
Air-to-Ground Voice Transcription (1970)

One of the biggest issues in software design and implementation is when the problem that needs to be solved is not completely and clearly defined. If this happens, several knock-on effects happen.

- How is the team supposed to write code if the goal and scope of the problem is not clearly defined?

- Unclear problem statements also lead to unsuccessful tests and code reviews. Indeed, how can you check for correctness (test) and cleanness (code reviews) of the code if you don't have a clear problem in mind that has been solved with a given piece of code?

- If you don't know what the project is supposed to do, how can you define whether or not a project or feature is done? By done, I mean done-done. Not *well I coded something.*

So, make sure you have a clearly defined problem statement. A clear problem statement ensures common understanding of the solutions to the problem.

A word of caution, done-done does not imply that a problem needs to be sorted in its entirety right away. Incremental solutions are gold for building the right solution, for progress, and for gathering feedback during the development process. However, the end goal and what (i.e., the *scope*) needs to be achieved in every increment should be clear.

Consider, for example, a car. Ideally, a company might want to provide different versions for a broad brand acquisition: manual and automatic shift, diesel or electric cars.

A car already takes a lot of increments to be assembled: building wheels, engines, and brakes, you name it. Trying to build all possible versions before even starting releasing a simple diesel manual super-basic car will make the company basically file for bankruptcy: it takes a lot of time, and you might end up with producing several variations of a car that customers do not like. What if all customers like a car with red wheels only? Wouldn't it be easier to have feedback after you built the first version (e.g., usable, safe) of the wheel? Fixing the wheel at this stage helps later in the process. Indeed, designing a single wheel and getting feedback and adoption before moving to other components avoids several issues like having produced 1,000 fully functioning cars to only then figure that you need to change wheels to all of them.

The same reasoning applies to the development process.

Is This Right?

Does the overall solution actually solve the problem? Looks trivial, but it is not. It might be easy enough to not have a clear plan of action to solve the real problem. Always have a clear view of the solution you want to achieve in the end, and carefully plan in advance how to break down everything to be there, on time.

If you are using lean methodologies, always have a clear *minimum viable product (MVP)*.

■ **Minimum Viable Product**   A minimum viable product is the smallest set of requirements and relative implementation that needs to be satisfied to start progressing toward the ultimate project goal, while providing a finite, usable functionality.

A word of caution is needed here anyway. Figure 6-1 shows how to correctly implement MVP iterations. Please, do not just ship functionalities. Always consider a nice slice up to the top of the pyramid. Indeed, instead of focusing on each layer bottom up (e.g., all functionalities first in the left pyramid), always consider each iteration (right pyramid):

- A piece of functionality
- Any reliability level that the small functionality you implemented needs
- Relevant usability
- The design on the smaller functionality implemented and how it fits in the broader view

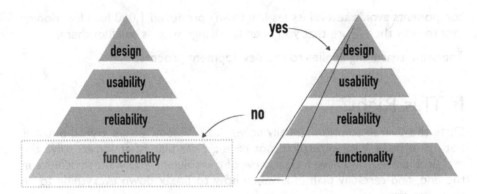

Figure 6-1. MVP dos and don'ts

Back to our example of building a car. While the pyramid on the left consists of building a possibly not tested basic car, the right one would build one piece at the time. Again, the wheel

- Is a piece of functionality.

- Needs to be reliable and safe to use.

- Must be usable. For example, a functioning and reliable wheel that does not fit the overall size of the vehicle is not really usable.

- And, as discussed, our clients really love red wheels. We have to be able to gather feedback and implement it sooner rather than later.

Have order, not entropy, moving each and every time a step closer to the goal: the entire software, clean and with all the right requirements and design executed.

Requirements

In this section, we describe the main requirements that need to be taken into account to understand whether or not we are solving the right problem in the correct manner.

Requirements are **functional** (i.e., *what* do we solve) and **nonfunctional** (i.e., *how* do we solve it). Even if they are high level and implementation independent, a review process is needed to ensure we are reaching the desired goal.

Since we are focusing on *good code*, in the following, we will expand our previous discussion on nonfunctional requirements, addressing it, however, from a higher-level perspective rather than implementation-specific point of view.

FURPS+

A common definition of nonfunctional requirements can be summarized by the acronym FURPS+,[1] which provides the following categories:

- **Functional**: Which includes features, capabilities, and security.

- **Usability**: Which includes human factor and human interactions, consistency in interfaces, context help for the user where required, and so on.

- **Reliability**: Which includes the impact of failures, how frequent they are and their severity, the recoverability, accuracy, and predictability of the system.

- **Performance**: Which includes efficiency, availability, throughput, accuracy, response time, and usage of resources—just to mention some.

- **Supportability**: Which includes how easy it is to test, extend, and maintain the system. It also includes other characteristics such as how flexible is the system in terms of adaptation to changes.

The + in the acronym indicates a set of additional requirements:

- **Implementation**: Including tools and languages as we will describe later.

- **Interfaces**: Imposed by external systems and/or legacy code.

- **Packaging**: Including constraints on how the system will actually be delivered.

- **Operations**: Including details on how the system will be actually administered once deployed.

- **Legal**: Including any legal requirements such as license and regulations.

■ **Note** The ultimate goal of using FURPS+, or any other model for requirements, is to make sure that you are taking a step away from the nitty-gritty details of code and technologies and have a chance to consider what the problem you are trying to solve is.

---

[1] Grady, R. B. Practical Software Metrics for Project Management and Process Improvement. Prentice Hall, Englewood Cliffs, NJ, USA, 1992.

Validation

Requirements are not only used, as we have seen so far, to validate internal implementation. They are also used to validate that what we offer is in check with clients/users needs and expectations.

The following properties are needed to perform a good validation process:

- **Completeness**: Requirements are complete if all possible scenarios (and features) are described.

- **Correctness**: Requirements are strictly intended for the contexts needed by the client/end user. No unintended features are described.

- **Consistency**: Two or more requirements can't contradict each other.

- **Unambiguity**: A requirement can't be interpreted in multiple manners.

- **Realistic**: The overall system can be implemented within the given constraints.

- **Verifiable**: Once implemented, the system can be verified (tested) in a repeatable way.

- **Traceable**: Every functionality, or intermediate artifact, can be traced back to its relative requirement.

■ **Note** The ultimate goal of validation is to make sure that the problem you modeled so far is feasible and that it cannot be misinterpreted. Finally, remember, a problem is solved by a project. According to *PMBOK*, 6th edition, a project is a temporary effort undertaken to provide unique value with a given scope on time and on a budget.[2] Validation ensures that you have a project at hand and hence the overall team is ensured progression and completion of the attainment of the requirements and its value.

Technologies

When evaluating if you are solving the right problem, question if the technologies, tools, libraries, and platforms (you name it) you are willing to use are adequate.

---

[2]Project Management Institute, *PMBOK Guide, Sixth Edition* (2017).

Choosing the right technologies comes with some key indicators:

- Use past **experience** as a reference, but do not blindly copy paste. Likewise in project management for cost/time estimation, a reference to previously used technologies to solve similar project might be used. However, we should never blindly think that since we used technology X in the past, it suits well the problem on hand.

- **Industry trends** might also be a reference. Anyway, just because it is a trend, it does not mean that it fits the specific requirements you have.

- If the code **needs** to be portable, scalable, and performing, take these aspects into account.

- Be open to **brainstorming**. Even the uttermost skilled person might find beneficial confronting with peers to identify gaps and opportunities.

- Do not stick with a certain approach just because you are emotionally attached to it.

- Avoid the **when you have a hammer, everything looks like a nail** mentality.

What Do You Have? What Do You Need?

When assessing the solution and the technologies you are willing to use to solve a given a problem and how it contributes to the overall software, always assess if the solution fits the problem you are solving.

In almost all scenarios, you will need to cooperate with several other programmers in the team. Assess the core skills both yourself and the team have or lack and how they fit into the overall solution that needs to be implemented. Is the solution feasible? Does the team have some weak points? In such case, work on thinking about the impact of such decisions. As an example:

- Does an equally good yet more viable solution exist?
- What is the learning curve of the given solution?
- What is the impact of the learning curve on the time it will take to develop the solution?

▓ **Note**   I am totally in for trying something and learning from it, even at the cost of risking failure. Hence, as part of growing as a programmer and as a team, I am not discouraging you from trying different things just because "we always did them in a certain way" or because of any learning curve. Learning is amazing. What I am suggesting is to be mindful about the existence of such potential constraints and to make informed decisions about the solutions you will ultimately strive for. This will make space for better and more productive brainstorming sessions and design with the entire team.

This aspect, between all, also impacts technological choices. For example, you might be setting up the project for failure if you suddenly decide to use a platform that your team is not comfortable (i.e., skilled) with. Evaluating alternatives is the way to go in the short term, as well as starting training others if the wonderful technology might be considered useful for future development. If the business allows so, hire experts in the field to speed up the growth curve.

▓ **Warning**   I am not discouraging learning or the introduction of new technologies when needed. The key point is to always think about trade-offs (e.g., fit for purpose vs. team knowledge) and the implications that such decisions imply for the broader team.

Processes

The last collateral aspect to consider when reviewing the overall software high-level design is about processes. They should always be

- Clear
- Complete
- Systematic

Most importantly, they should be actionable and aimed at moving forward in the direction of having *manageable* development. As a personal consideration, I suggest to not mix and match aspects from different methodologies within the same project. Some projects might run better with agile, while others with an iterative or a spiral approach. Always have them clearly defined and stick with them.

▓ **Note**   I do not mean for you to not try and experiment how to improve processes. If, for example, you figure that agile approaches suit better your development process rather than a waterfall, you should definitely make a switch, learn, and evaluate the improvements obtained. However, strive for long-term consistency.

Approach for Code Reviews

I want to give you an approach template to help you out during design reviews. Always think about reviews as a lifecycle on its own within the SDLC as shown in Figure 6-2.

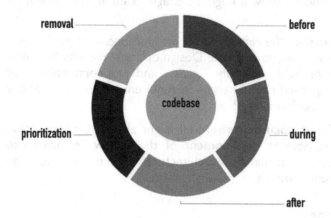

Figure 6-2. Code reviews lifecycle

The *before* phase sets the stage for the review and what it will focus on. *During* is the actual code review phase. It requires some extra steps to be performed to ensure a successful and actionable review. The *after* phase helps in summarizing the findings of the review and provides enough details to the following *prioritization* of defects and their *removal*.

Before You Start

As anticipated, it is really important to apply the same planning concepts and clarity of what code needs to be implemented to code reviews as well. In the following, a set of fields useful to think about before a review can be started:

- **Project name**: Project name.
- **Reviewer**: Person in charge of performing the review.
- **Technical contact**: Person responsible for the project (e.g., gatekeeper).
- **Name of developer(s)**: All the developers involved in the project.
- **Review scope**: Enter the review with a specific scope. Are you reviewing all the components? A subsystem? System of systems? Make it clear and well defined.

- *Review number*: Keep track of the number of review iteration performed.

- *Date of review*: Date of the review.

- *Date of the previous review*: Date of the previous review. I know it might be tough to admit how time went by.

- *Goal of the review*: What are the specific objectives you are trying to evaluate? Design options? Fix what's broken approach? Identify gaps and opportunities for improvement? Changes in requirements (e.g., scalability or performance)?

- *Input documentation*: Highlight all the documentation available at the moment of the review, including use cases, scenarios, architecture documentation, and requirements.

In Progress

This phase provides extra steps to be performed during reviews. Likewise you would document the code (do you?) as we will discuss in Chapter 8, it is critical, for analogous reasons, to not rush the review process and take some time to document your findings step by step. Specifically, for each portion of code under review, always document

- *Number of defects*: Number of the issues found with the review.

- *Impact*: Always rank the impact a defect is having on the overall project's quality (e.g., minor, medium, high, critical). This will help you out after the review to schedule improvement actions.

After

This is a very critical step, especially for broad reviews like a design one. Always consider to

- Provide more details for the improvements needed.

- Provide trade-offs and suggestions when possible.

Completing the review with these last steps will better support the team in doing the required adjustment.

After all this documentation, indeed, better and more informed decisions can be made on how to prioritize the resolution of defects and how to keep up with new code in development while acting upon the findings of code reviews.

■ **Heads Up**   Chapter 11 will wrap up both the review and the software development lifecycles together.

Summary

In this chapter, we went a step higher in the abstraction of a problem and relative review. Specifically, we considered how to look at a problem and relative requirements to ensure that

1.   You are solving the right problem.

2.   All constraints and ultimate goal are clear, not ambiguous and feasible.

3.   Technological and process choices speed up and maximize the effort toward success, instead of hindering it.

The main takeaway is to not think about reviews only at development time (e.g., with peer reviews). Embed them at the very early stages of the SDLC. A good start ensures a successful end.

In the next chapter, we will start considering some general guidelines that can and needs to be implemented in any type of code review. Specifically, we will introduce conventions for data and naming.

Further Reading

If you are intrigued about properly thinking about general problems and the frameworks used in project management, definitely read PMI's PMBOK Guide. Some concepts and flows are very specific to the art of management, of course. But having at least a quick glance at it will help in having a well-structured approach on how to think about the development process and the phases every project should go through.

Code Review Checklist

1. Does the overall design meet the requirements?

2. Is the design realistic and feasible in terms of time needed to be implemented (especially in initial phases of development)?

3. Are interfaces well suited to deal with both internal and external interactions?

4. Are design principles agreed, shared, and cohesive?

5. Is the problem statement properly defined?

6. Is the design actually solving the issues within the problem statement?

7. Is the FURPS+ model (or similar) taken into account?

8. Is usability (end-user perspective) considered?

9. Is reliability considered?

10. Are performances properly described at high level?

11. Is supportability with all its facets considered?

12. Are operational requirements defined and met?

13. Are packaging constraints defined and met? This includes how the code is supposed to be released in production.

14. Are legal requirements considered? This is, for example, the case of code released publicly without a proper consideration of intellectual property and the processes around it. It is also the case of any possible copyright infringement from libraries or data reuse.

15. Are requirements complete?

16. Are they correct?

17. Are requirements consistent?

18. Is ambiguity removed from them?

19. Is the specification realistic?

20. Is it verifiable?

21. Can be requirements traced back to their relative functionalities?

22. Are technologies, platforms, languages, libraries, and tools adequate?

23. Does the team have the expertise required to advance the project?

24. Are the processes in place complete and actually manageable?

25. Is the definition of done appropriate?

26. Is the minimum viable product (MVP) clearly defined?

27. Is MVP properly defined (i.e., not only functionalities)?

28. Does the design show signs of serial hammering?

29. Have industry trends and previous experience been thoughtfully considered?

30. Is the team skilled based on the project requirements and technologies?

31. Is training needed?

32. Does the team have the necessary skills?

33. What is the impact of any learning curve to the execution of the project?

34. Are findings from the review process properly documented?

Naming and Formatting Conventions

There is nothing more deceptive than an obvious fact.

—Sherlock Holmes in Sir Arthur Conan Doyle's
"The Boscombe Valley Mystery" (1891)

In theory, declaring a variable is a child's play:

```
i_am_a_var = 10
```

Sure enough it gets the job done: having a variable ready for use as you wish.

However, picking naming right can add (or remove) a lot from the overall quality of the code you write. A clear and consistent naming scheme, as subtle it might seem at first, will play you well in the short, medium, and long run. Indeed, haphazard names lead to confusion, highly impacting readability and maintainability of the codebase.

© Giuliana Carullo 2020
G. Carullo, *Implementing Effective Code Reviews*,
https://doi.org/10.1007/978-1-4842-6162-0_7

This chapter quickly describes common dos and don'ts and guidelines on how to look at naming when building clean code. It is not a matter of *"you have to"* approach. But it takes less effort to implement these good practices than reviewing or trying to understand the code later on. Thus, *"you really should"* implement them.

We are also going to quickly introduce good practices around the use of parameters and access modifiers as well as spacing since they all contribute to a well-rounded readable code.

Naming

As human beings, we all get a name at our birth. Our parents chose our names with love to welcome us in the world. Our name affects our life and how we interact with the world. We need to do the same with our baby code.

We already agreed that a lot of times we get so emotional with our baby code, and we want to take care of it. And choosing the right naming is just another way to show our code some love: "welcome on board, my code!" Choose wisely.

■ **Note** Bob, Mary, and Joe are wonderful names. When I speak about *baby code*, let's avoid these names for code, okay?

You Should Be... What?

Ambiguous names make the code hard to read. Not too short. Not too long. But you should be able to tell what they do at glance.

```
my_dict = dict()
```

In this example, there is no context that can help your future self, and other programmers, understand what the purpose of the dictionary is.

Hence, a first check is to ensure that chosen names are meaningful within the considered context. If names are meaningful and context oriented, they are easier to remember and eventually to look after.

Back to our example. Suppose you are modeling the age of a set of people, a more meaningful declaration would be

```
users_age = dict()
```

How not to do context orientation:

- Don't try to be funny. If you are happy, you can't name your variable *lol* or *rotfl*. As much as I am a big believer in having some fun, do not compromise the meaningfulness of a name just for the fun of it. You won't be laughing later on when you cannot remember the enjoyment at that time, nor when other programmers will enquire you about it. It is also highly probable that it will not make it through any peer review process.

- Don't be shy and use single letter variable names. If you feel shy or speechless, you still can't use *a*, *g*, or *m*. Indexing with *i*, *j*, or *k* is totally okay. That's it. These are, generally, the only single context-oriented single letter variable names allowed. Bonus: you are allowed to use *n* for loops.

- Don't try to impress other programmers using acronyms to express the context. TVMNTM stands for *"this variable means nothing to me."* It is context oriented. Oh well, don't use it.

Note Indexes (i, j, k) are okay in loops. Nonetheless, more descriptive names always help, especially for multiple nested loops.

Not You Again

Not the same thing is declared with different names, not same name for different things.

Back to our previous example:

```
my_dict = dict()
```

It is not only a matter of readability and longer-term memory. Getting into the habit of not using meaningful names often leads to scattering the same name over and over across the codebase. This would make code readers even more confused and having a harder time to understand what a variable is used for, what is the context, and the scope it lives in.

Takeaway Always pick meaningful names. It will help readability and maintainability, especially in large-scale software.

Keywords

Certain languages, like Python, allow us to use keywords as variable names. Consider the example in the following. Python offers several built-in functions. *type( )* is one of them that given an object as argument returns its type:

```
type(3)
>>> <type 'int'>
```

The interpreter would not be mad at you if you use type as variable name; indeed, the following snippet of code is okay and runs with no apparent issue:

```
type = 5
print (type)
>>> 5
```

What if at a later stage in your code you remember that you need the built-in function instead? The code won't work, because now type is referencing an *int* object instead.

```
type(3)

>>> Traceback (most recent call last):
  File "<stdin>", line 1, in <module>
TypeError: 'int' object is not callable
```

■ **Takeaway** Long story short, keywords are reserved to the language. Do not use them.

The Good, the Bad, the Ugly

Switching between different languages can make it difficult to follow naming conventions.

In this section, we are going to explore some Python conventions. However, before writing your very first line of code, always go and check the convention for your language.

Let's go through each one.

■ **Refresher** Private members are only accessible locally (e.g., within a class). Protected members are visible both locally (same class) and by any subclass.

Variables, functions, and packages names should not use camel case, and words should be separated by underscores:

```
something_like_this
```

Private methods start with double underscore:

```
__i_am_a_secret_agent(self, params)
```

Protected methods start with single underscore:

```
_i_am_a_protected_method(self, params)
```

■ **Heads Up** Context specific applies. Always think in advance if a class is meant to be extended (i.e., used for inheritance) and, hence, about its implications on public or private variables. Default behavior should always be to consider a component private, unless clearly needed to be used as protected or public.

Use CamelCase for classes and exceptions:

```
BrandNewClass(object)
```

Constants are always all caps separated by underscores:

```
I_AM_A_CONSTANT = 'whatever whatever'
```

And always use *reverse_notation* for multi-worded names used within the same context.

The good:

```
element_a = 'whatever a'
element_b = 'whatever b'
element_c = 'whatever c'
```

The bad:

```
a_element = 'whatever a'
b_element = 'whatever b'
c_element = 'whatever c'
```

How's *the ugly*?

Well, when names are not grouped based on context, it's ugly.

▨ **Bonus Tip**   If you can't find a proper name for a new method, class, and so on, ensure that you are not dealing with a *bossy component.*

Python Naming Conventions in Short

This section provides a quick recap of naming conventions for Python.[1] Specifically

- Packages and modules names are all lower case. Underscores can be present for readability purposes if multiple words are present. Filenames are treated like a module; hence, same naming conventions apply.

- Classes are CamelCase. Exceptions are treated as classes and hence follow the same naming convention.

- Functions and variables are lower case, separated with underscore if multiple words are present. If a variable is local—by definition—it does not need any underscore to signal access type.

- Constants are all caps, separated with underscores if needed.

Table 7-1 provides a quick reference for the most common naming conventions and their use depending on the desired (if any) visibility.

Table 7-1. Naming Conventions Summary

Type	Convention	Public	Protected	Private
Package	Lower case	lower_case	-	-
Module	Lower case	lower_case	-	-
Filename	Lower case	lower_case.txt	-	-
Class	Camel case	CamerCase()	-	-
Exception	Camel case	CamelCase()	-	-
Function	Lower case	lower_case()	_lower_case()	__lower_case()
Variable	Lower case	lower_case	_lower_case	__lower_case
Local variable	Lower_case	-	-	lower_case
Constant	All caps	ALL_CAPS	_ALL_CAPS	__ALL_CAPS

---

[1] www.python.org/dev/peps/pep-0008/#naming-conventions

That's Magic

```
MAGIC_NUMBER = 42
```

Even if 42 is the answer to the ultimate question of life, the universe, and everything, it is not a good practice.

As much as I would love to ignore 42 as a magic number in the code review because I am a geek at heart, magic numbers should be considered with caution and avoided if possible.

They are not a good practice because their meaning is often hard to link back to the actual context.

Suppose that for whatever reason (if you did it, please let me know why) you are trying to put *The Hitchhiker's Guide to Galaxy* into code format. A probably better named constant would be

```
LIFE_UNIVERSE_EVERYTHING = 42
```

■ **Savage Hardcoding**   If you can, avoid hardcoding like the plague. If you really have to use it, make sure it is minimal and easy to locate (i.e., not scattered all over the codebase). Furthermore, any use of hardcoding is tight back to meaningful names.

Parameterization

In simple words, passing too many arguments as input to functions and methods is not a good idea. Here's an example:

```
def too_many_params(first, second, third, fourth, ... , nth):
    ...
```

It makes the code less readable and it might make testing trickier. The suggested options to solve this type of defect are

1. Use optional parameters if possible.

2. Consider—if it is sound—to create a new class that contains the input parameters. Thus, pass the single instance as input to the function/method.

Consider the following example:

```
def update_and_store_account(id, name, surname, username, preferences, ...):
    ...
```

It would be far better designed by specifying an *account* class that maintains all the parameter:

```
class Account(object):
...
    def _init_(self, id, name, surname, username,  preferences, ...):
        self._id = id
        self._name = name
        self._surname = surname
        self._username = username
        self._preferences = preferences
        ...
...
```

■ **Takeaway**   When writing or reviewing parameters, look at how many of them are in place for each component. Always consider options to reorganize and reduce their appearance as input for a single component. Too many parameters might be also a signal for a bigger problem to be looked at (i.e., design smells). Indeed, it might be the case of having too many parameters because the code is breaking the single responsibility principle.

Modifiers

Access modifiers also play an important role in readable code as well as maintaining the overall design and architecture sound.

You might be used to Java, where encapsulation dominates everything. Python, au contraire, is less strict on this aspect.

"But wait, Giuliana," you say, "you told me that for private methods I should use double underscore."

That is called name mangling, which leads to potentially treating each of the methods as public. But I wouldn't. If methods have been made private, it means that someone specifically designed them in such a way that signals that you should not access them from the outside. In this case, indeed, the private method might be just temporary; its signature might change in the future or even change its inner behavior. This would cost changes to all the callers and lots of headaches.

■ **Note**   If I haven't convinced you so far, at least, respect the will of previous programmers.

Formatting Code

Spacing properly is also important to achieve uniform and readable code. In the following some guidance on most common practices.

Line Spacing

Like naming, spacing properly helps in achieving readable code. General guidance for Python code includes

- Two vertical spaces ahead of classes. Since a class gathers together a single behavior, spacing is performed accordingly to place more emphasis on responsibilities separation.

- One vertical space for class methods.

- No line separation within the same method.

Note If you are tempted to add several blank lines into a single method, it might be an early indicator of a method being too long and possibly breaking the single responsibility principle.

Indentation

While line spacing creates visual separation between logically separated behaviors vertically, indentation does it horizontally and deals also with grouping of logical statements. General rule of thumb for Python code is as follows:

- Always use four whitespaces to define a block (e.g., loop, code at class level, method level, conditional flow)

- Tabs are generally preferred over spaces. However, consistency is important. If most of the codebase uses already four consecutive spaces instead of tabs, it is okay to keep using them, but strive for consistency.

Whitespace

Readability can be improved even down to a single-line statement. This is the case, for example, of properly spacing boolean operators into a conditional statement. General guidance is the following:

- Add a whitespace on both sides of boolean, comparison, and assignment operators.

- Like natural language for parentheses and punctuation. This implies

  - No space immediately after an open parenthesis and no space immediately before a closing parenthesis

  - Space after a comma, but no space before it

- No space at the end of each line (known as *trailing space*)

Python Spacing in Short

Properly spacing down to every line of code helps ensure readable code and adds semantic cues of separation to programmers reading the code.

Table 7-2 provides a summary of spacing conventions.

Table 7-2. Spacing Conventions Summary

Type	Convention
Class	Two blank lines before
Function and method	Single blank line before
Block within function	No blank line
Boolean, comparison, and assignment operators	Whitespace both sides
End of line	No space
Code indentation	Tab (four spaces)
Parenthesized expressions	No spaces immediately after and before inside the expression
Comma	No space before, single space after

Here it is a final word on spacing and whitespaces: as almost everything in life, too much of something might cause the opposite effect of the wanted goal. The same applies to spacing. Adding too many whitespaces can decrease readability instead of improving it.

Summary

In this chapter, we provided guidelines and examples around common naming problems and their impact on clean code.

As explained in this chapter

- Naming has a big impact on the readability of the code.

- Plenty of factors including parameterization, access modifiers, keywords, and hardcoding need to be considered for a well-rounded code review.

A general takeaway is that conventions are not always strictly enforced. When in doubt, check the reference guide, and if no guidance is provided on a specific aspect, at the very least, ensure that naming choices are consistent across the codebase.

In the next chapter, we will provide more guidance on commenting the code, why it is important and how to make the best use of it.

■ **Heads Up**   Many of the guidelines described in this chapter can be automated. Specifically, tools for automated PEP8 checks exist: consider tools already in place within your company or pick the one that best suits your needs and preferences.

Further Reading

If you want a laugh, check out "How To Write Unmaintainable Code" by Andrew Yurisich (https://github.com/Droogans/unmaintainable-code). It is a quick and nice reference on unmaintainable code. PEP8 (www.python. org/dev/peps/pep-0008/#naming-conventions) provides a comprehensive guide on Python guidelines for naming.

Review Checklist

1. Are redundant parameters present in the class (might be the case of instance var instead)?

2. Does the code follow the naming conventions of the chosen language (e.g., CamelCase for Java)?

3. Are names of variable, methods, and classes meaningful?

4. Are names of variable, methods, and classes descriptive?

5. Are names consistent across the codebase?

6. Are names context oriented?

7. Are keywords used for variable naming?

8. Can you understand from the function/method/class/variable name what is it expected to perform?

9. Are too many parameters in place?

10. Are optional parameters adequately used?

11. Are modifiers used appropriately?

12. Are global variables in place? Are they actually needed?

13. Does the code contain magic numbers?

14. Is abstraction by parameterization achieved?

15. Is parameterization needed to remove redundancies?

16. Are generic types used when needed to improve reusability (Java)?

17. Is naming giving insights of a bossy component?

18. Are private methods called from the outside (Python)?

19. Are spacing conventions respected?

Comments

I listen to their story, they listen to my comments, and then I pocket my fee.

—Sherlock Holmes in Sir Arthur Conan Doyle's
"A Study in Scarlet" (1887)

I know you probably mumbled several times while coding because you have been asked to write or to update comments. You might think, is it not enough to have some sort of comments inside my code? They must be coherent as well? Mumble, mumble. The answer is yes, they have to. Think about it as doing a favor for your future self. Months from now, you may need to revisit the code you wrote today. It might be crystal clear to you right now, but will you remember why you used variable *XYZ* a week from now? Probably. But how about a few months from now? Unlikely.

We will discuss in this chapter more in detail the reasons why good comments are still needed to support good code and how to achieve them. Good comments, like naming, help in making the code more readable and quicker to understand.

Indeed, good comments help

- New team members to get up to speed with the code, no matter how experienced they are.

- External (to the team) collaborators. Assume you are trying to better understand dependencies to/from software outside your team's ownership. The very last

© Giuliana Carullo 2020
G. Carullo, *Implementing Effective Code Reviews*,
https://doi.org/10.1007/978-1-4842-6162-0_8

thing you want to do is having to read all the code to understand it. Sure you would not read comments piece by piece. However, an overarching documentation for every considerable piece of software is mandatory.

- Any programmer, really. There is no single way to implement a functionality, even the simplest one. A solution obvious to one programmer might be not that obvious to another one. Good comments help to better understand reasoning around it.

"If the Code Is Good, I Don't Need Comments" Philosophy

If the code is good, I don't need comments.

This philosophy is partially true, having a good piece of code surely is the way to go (at the end of the day, well-written code is all this book is about). However, this philosophy might be applicable for a very small codebase.

As soon as the code grows in size, you might end up reading the code line by line for each and every piece you need to build upon. What if the code is well written but still implements complex algorithms? And if also naming is not on track, you are setting up your future self and your colleagues for failure.

Far away from recommending pages-long comments, but they should be in place and well written (as described in the following sections), even for good code. As a plus, people will complain about poorly documented code; they will not complain about more verbose descriptions.

■ **Takeaway** Well-written code is not an excuse to avoid adding comments altogether.

Conditions and Flows

Comments serve the purpose of specifying how the method/procedure performs its task. They are not meant to punish so-so code writers. Comments are a way to succinctly abstract the inner work of your code in common language. And supplementing comments with pre- and post-conditions is beneficial.

▓ **Note**   As anticipated, there is no single solution for any piece of code. Providing good descriptions for pre- and post-conditions helps other programmers to better understand why the software has been written in a specific way. This is especially helpful for programmers fairly new to the business logic comments referred to.

A **pre-condition** is defined as a set of conditions that need to hold true when the method or function is called. A **post-condition** is a statement describing the condition after the method or function has performed its duties.

Embedding them into your comments is not only beneficial from a readability perspective, but it will also help during test design. Consider, for example, the scenario in which you have a subset of the team strictly focusing on designing and developing tests. In this case, it will be surely cost saving for them to have specified exactly the conditions that need to hold true before and after a call. It will be definitely faster and easier for them to check for edge cases and possible errors and design overall better and more complete test cases.

Clear pre- and post-conditions also help in defining the **flow** (i.e., the logic) of the block of code. What to expect? Documenting the flow should also include any raised exception. Yes, please, I definitely want to know if the code I am using could explode at a certain point.

▓ **Takeaway**   Add context to your methods. Shortly, but clearly, comment any pre- and post-condition as well as a flow brief and any exception that the code might raise.

IO Definition

Comments should clearly document the type of input(s) and output(s). This is especially true for dynamically typed languages like Python. Let's look at the following code snippet. It is an example of both so-so naming and confusion created by missing defined types into the documentation:

```python
def add(first, second):
    #method body
    ...
```

It is pretty clear that the method is performing an add operation. However, the type of the inputs is not clear.

Are these operands? Are they integers? Float numbers? Strings? Is the method performing more complex operations on data structures? The parameter *first* might be a dictionary, a list, or anything else, and it might be performing more complex operations to add the parameter *second* to it. Or they might be both data structures, and the method is adding the elements from the second data structures to the first one.

Yes, you might read the code to understand the inputs' types. Is it the most effective solutions? In this case, the snip pet of code is simple, so yes it takes a short amount of time to check it out. Otherwise, we are back to the consequences of the "If the code is good, I don't need comments" philosophy.

You might also think, "Well... if I improve the names of the parameters (first and second), I can avoid writing comments?"

The answer is still probably no. What happens to the abstraction power of the method? What about its reusability? It might be context dependent, of course. But the rule of thumb is clearly stating the IO's types.

▓ **Takeaway**   Clearly state and document input/output types.

Inline Comments

Too many inline comments instead of—as an example—a clear comment on top of the method drive me crazy. This does not mean to avoid inline comments at all costs. They should be present where actually needed. Anyway, when a method can be effectively described with *docstrings*, I would definitely go for this option.

From time to time, too many inline comments might also hint other issues within the code. Indeed, it might be the case of a too complex, too long, more than a single feature implemented by the code. When it is not easy to shortly and effectively describe the code you wrote, check again the code. Is it implementing just one feature? Is it too long? Might it be split? If so, you have more than a single defect to fix.

▓ **Takeaway**   Use inline comments, but do so sparingly.

TODOs

Inline comments are also used to signal a block of code that needs to be debugged, tested, or generally improved. In other words, they are the handy *TODO* and *FIX-ME* comments we all introduce in our code to avoid breaking the process of writing our most creative, productive piece of coding art.

A nice piece of craft could be

```
def my_magnificent_method():
    # TODO: comment me, Giuliana said so
    ...
```

Even if I would love to read such code, please don't wait a decade before fixing any TODO and FIX-ME comments. They are meant to be temporary, and they should remain so. Even more, no TODOs and FIX ME in the code you are somehow releasing.

■ **Note**   TODOs and the alike can be okay if you use them temporarily in code running locally and possibly a shared staging environment. However, the recommendation is to not have them leaking into production code: they quickly compound as technical debt does.

That's Obvious

Writing comments is good. Writing good comments is tremendous! However, commenting also obvious things is not appropriate. If the code is really simple, there is no need for commenting each and every line of it. Consider the following example:

```
...
# gets the glossary of the book
glossary = book.get_glossary()
# check the keywords we are looking for
if keyword in glossary:
    # return the associated definition
    return glossary[keyword]
else:
    # return None since the keyword is not in glossary
    return None
...
```

It is obvious what the code is doing, and good variable naming helps a lot. A better commenting style would be

```
...
# Returns the definition for a keyword if it exists.
# None otherwise.
glossary = book.get_glossary()
if keyword in glossary:
    return glossary[keyword]
else:
    return None
...
```

It is much more readable, isn't it?

Takeaway   Adding comments for every line of code is an overkill: no programmer needs an English translation of the entire codebase.

Did You Just Lie to That programmer?

Comments are intrinsically virtuous and worthy of reward. They really are. Writing good comments such that it is easy for a programmer to understand the functionality and just glance over it while lying is a big no-no.

If you write top-notch comments, but you lie in them, I appreciate your sense of humor. I really do. But please, don't.

Jokes aside, it might be the case where comments and documentation have not been updated accordingly to the evolution of code, hence resulting in not being coherent.

Not properly maintained comments and documentation are probably even worse than having no comments at all: it is misleading. Do not use it as an excuse, but as a programmer, I would rather be unwillingly confronted with the truth of having to read the entire code to understand it, rather than eventually exploring a big code base trusting documentation to end up puzzled and going back and forth to figure out that:

1.   Documentation has not been maintained.

2.   Regardless of the existence of documentation, I have to read and explore the actual code to understand what a component does.

3.   Rethinking and understanding the big picture again.

Takeaway   Maintaining comments and documentation is an integrated part of writing code: do not leave it behind.

Subtle Hints

Just on a safe side, comments describe current code *only*.

Please, resist any urge to use comments to describe how better and shiner your new solution is compared to the previously developed code.

The key goal of developing software, as well as performing reviews, is to make the code incrementally better.

Think about a codebase that existed for 10 years and hundreds of people touched and improved it over time. If every engineer had to document how they contributed to the code compared to the previous version, we would end up with a novel of improvements and complaints rather than a clear and readable codebase.

■ **Takeaway**   Nobody benefits from comments that are not descriptive of current code and **only** current code.

Typos

Do not feel guilty if you added some typos (e.g., misspelling or grammar errors) in comments or documentation. We are human and it happens to all of us. However, they should be treated like any bug or piece of technical debt: the sooner they are fixed, the better.

Between all the bad things happening in the world, they are the tiniest thing if we put them in context. However, they do speak about personal branding (as a programmer) and can quickly escalate to the company brand.

Consider the best piece of code with typos in the documentation. Fortunately enough it is a customer facing. (Yay! Someone use it!) Unfortunately enough, the customer will notice the typo, will cringe a little bit, and potentially make wrongful conclusions to the quality of the code as well.

They can also add frustration. Consider, for example, the scenario where an error or exception containing typos is raised. Errors are frustrating on their own; let's imagine if they are even more tricky to understand due to misspelling or grammar errors.

Lucky days, fixing typos is super quick and easy, and if you have any type of review in place, it is easy to catch them.

■ **Takeaway**   I hear you; almost everyone dislikes when someone judges an entire book by its cover. Yet, it does happen. It happens for books. It happens with CVs when you apply for a job. It happens to documentation. We live in a world where the brain is constantly overwhelmed with way too much information and, often, decisions need to be made quickly. A small thing like typos goes a long way in the image of the code we portray. Use reviews to make sure they do not get seen by more eyeballs.

The Economy of Entire Words

Don't be too quick to judge me saying that I am too old, yet, but do not use texting abbreviations in your comments and documentation.

My age forced me to live the broad adoption of the first mobile phones. I lived and observed the trend of words shrinking down to fit a single SMS.

Times evolved and we are definitely not charged anymore for the amount of characters we use in text messages. Hence, the only real need for using text abbreviations is gone for good.

Please do not use texting abbreviations in any form or shape, comments included.

Comments-Driven Development (CDD)

Comments-driven development (CDD) is centered on writing plain text description of the code first and then the actual implementation. They help in brainstorming the solution, setting clear inputs and outputs, and describing the kind of functionality that is going to be implemented.

As an analogy, think about teaching something to someone. In order to properly express in natural language a certain concept, you have to have a good understanding of it. The same happens with CDD: you are able to write the comment only if you properly thought about what that piece of code is going to implement.

Furthermore, oftentimes we are so inspired that we start compulsively typing lines and lines of code, to discover, only in the end, that we have to travel back in time to remember what they were supposed to do.

Even if I don't think implementing CDD is an absolute must, it can be handy.

Takeaway   Especially if you have serious commenting issues, try to explore CDD as a possible approach for your development process.

Coding Conventions

Some coding conventions like PEP8 (Python Software Foundation) for Python impose the presence of docstrings only for public modules, functions, classes, and methods. They remain optional for private or protected, where usually a comment after the function signature still describes the method.

As soon as you become aware of the language you are going to use for your project, check coding conventions and stick with them.

■ **Takeaway**   When entering a new coding environment and switching programming language, always check and implement from the start the coding conventions provided by the given language.

Final Tips on Documentation

If comments are properly written, you would be surprised how much investing a few more minutes during the development process would impact positively writing the overall documentation for the code.

Tools like Sphinx (www.sphinx-doc.org/en/master/) and the alike exist to automatically generate documentation from comments. Do it once; use it twice.

Summary

In this chapter, we introduced some common errors and misconceptions when approaching comments, and we provided guidance on how to use them properly so that they contribute to an overall clean and readable codebase.

Key takeaways

- Comments, and documentation in general, are quick to write as part of the development software. They should not be an afterthought.

- They help any programmer to quickly understand the code without having to read it all.

- They reduce the learning curve for new programmers.

Next, we will start analyzing key elements of design when approaching scenarios that require concurrency and parallelism.

Further Reading

Above all, *Clean Code* by Martin C. Fowler is one of the best resources written on the topic. I highly suggest this book as a general reference for your studies on how to write quality code.

PEP257 (www.python.org/dev/peps/pep-0257/), instead, provides detailed guidance on the use of docstrings for Python code.

Refresher   Docstrings are documentation strings added to the first line of methods, functions, and classes. They provide a handy way to add documentation to the code.

Review Checklist

1. Are comments coherent with the function/method/class they describe?

2. Are comments complete?

3. Are pre- and post-conditions properly described?

4. Are exceptions and errors documented?

5. Are input and output clearly defined and documented?

6. Is it clear (or otherwise commented) the type(s) of the input(s)?

7. Is it clear (or otherwise commented) the type(s) of the outputs?

8. Are all the flows of a method described (including errors/exceptions)?

9. Are TODOs, FIX-ME, and similar comments still present in released code?

10. Too many inline comments, are they needed?

11. Are comments easy to maintain over time?

12. Are coding conventions enforced?

13. Are obvious comments avoided?

14. Are comments and documentation well maintained?

15. Are comments used to describe current code only?

16. Do comments and documentation contain typos?

17. Is the commenting style in line with language guidelines (e.g., PEP8 for Python)?

Concurrency, Parallelism, and Performances

Little things are infinitely the most important.

—Sherlock Holmes in Sir Arthur Conan Doyle's
"A Case of Identity" (1891)

Let's be clear: concurrency and parallelism are not exactly the same thing.

Concurrency is the execution of multiple independent and interleaving pieces of computation. Concurrent programming ensures that their composition is correct, by means of handling the need for simultaneous access to shared resources.

Parallelism distinguishes itself by having these independent computations execute *simultaneously*.

Concurrency allows to structure the code in independent tasks to be performed that need coordination and communication between each other.

© Giuliana Carullo 2020
G. Carullo, *Implementing Effective Code Reviews*,
https://doi.org/10.1007/978-1-4842-6162-0_9

The underlying idea is that making better independent processes work in a coordinated fashion might help in speeding up the computation. And this is true, with the right assumptions.

I am pretty sure that all of us tried at least once in our life to implement a multi-threaded application that was actually slower than its sequential version. In this chapter, we will cover the foundations of concurrent and parallel programming and what to consider in terms of performances.

Foundation of Concurrency

So far we mainly focused on classical sequential programs. Nowadays, however, we like to exploit concurrency—that is, multiple tasks executed simultaneously fighting with each other for resources to try to speed up the execution time.

This section provides underlying knowledge around concurrent programming and highlights some basic mechanisms we need to ensure in our code to make it function correctly.

CPUs and Cores

CPUs and cores both serve the purpose of providing computation. However, they act at different levels (Table 9-1).

They both follow the *fetch, decode, and execute (FDE)* pattern, where

- **Fetch** gathers instructions from memory.
- **Decode** what instructions need to be performed.
- **Execute** the instruction.

Table 9-1. CPU vs. Core: Differences

CPU	Core
Fetch, decode, execute	Fetch, decode, execute
Circuit in a computer	Circuit in a CPU
Multiple CPUs in a computer	Multiple core in a CPU

However, a core is the basic computational unit within a CPU. CPUs can have, depending on the architecture, multiple cores. Similarly, computers can have multiple CPUs.

Usually, multicore architectures are known to be faster. However, just adding cores and/or CPUs does not make execution faster per se. We will explain it more in depth later in this chapter.

Threads Are Not Processes

Processes are the tools that the operating systems use to run programs. *Threads* are mini-blocks of code (sub-tasks) that can run within a process. In other words, a process can have multiple threads within it.

Threads use *shared memory* (processes don't) and they cannot execute code at the same time. Indeed, processes have their own execution environment, including own memory space. As a consequence, sharing information at process level is slower than sharing it at thread level. However, thread communication requires a deeper look at design phase.

Correctness of Concurrent Code

Two main properties ensure that concurrent code is correct: *safety* and *liveness*.

Safety is the property that ensures that nothing *"bad"* will happen. Liveness, on the other hand, ensures that something *"good"* will eventually happen.

Safety includes

- *Mutual exclusion*: Which means that two processes cannot *interleave* a certain sequence of lines of code (instructions).

- *Absence of deadlock*: A deadlock happens when two or more processes are blocking each other. This happens if each of them is waiting for the release of a given resource (e.g., a file) from the others.

Liveness is generally more difficult than safety to verify, since—as we will see in more details in the following—it depends on the scheduling of concurrent processes. It includes ensuring

- Absence of *starvation*: In case of starvation, a process could wait indefinitely and never run.

- *Fairness*: Which specifies how requests are handled and served.

Thread Safety

Thread safety is a property needed to guarantee correctness in concurrent software programs. As explained in the *"Foundation of Concurrency"* section, threads use **shared memory** (namely, **critical region** or **critical section**) that needs to be accessed in a mutually exclusive manner.

In other words, assume two threads T1 and T2 are trying to gain access to the critical section. By ensuring mutual exclusion, only one at a time can access the section as shown in Figure 9-1.

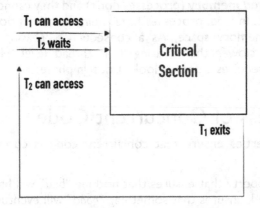

Figure 9-1. Mutual exclusion

Locks (https://docs.python.org/2.0/lib/lock-objects.html) are a common mechanism used to ensure mutual exclusion by using acquire() and release() functions to surround and control the critical section.

Generally speaking, an object is defined **thread safe** if, when accessed by multiple threads, its execution is correct, independently from thread's interleaving or scheduling.

Thus, concurrent access needs to be carefully managed. Indeed, between all, as anticipated, using locking mechanisms is not enough: we also need to ensure the absence of deadlocks. In our example, a deadlock happens if the critical section is free, but neither T1 nor T2 can access it.

A famous deadlock example is the dining philosophers problem (Figure 9-2). Legend has it that five philosophers met to eat and think with four forks available. Each of them tried to grab the right fork at the same time or think if the fork was not available. The problem they had was that they would not release the fork until both lunch and thinking ended, leaving one of them thinking and starving.

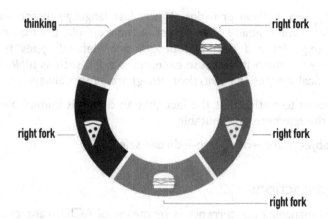

Figure 9-2. Dining philosophers problem

In the example, our philosophers are threads, while the fork is the shared resource. We can quickly deduct that a common cause of a deadlock happening is because of a lock (hence the access to the shared resource) not being properly released.

Note In Python, a context manager can be used to limit the possibility of a deadlock from happening.

When correctness depends on scheduling and interleaving times, like the dining philosophers problem, we have a *race condition*.

Immutable and Stateless

In object-oriented programming (OOP), objects can be mutable or immutable. Intuitively, immutable objects can't change their state after their creation.

As a consequence, immutable objects are thread safe. However, checking if an object is actually immutable when ensuring thread safety is non-negligible and oftentimes more tricky than expected.

As an example, an immutable object in Java is an object such that

- Its state cannot be changed after creation.
- All fields are declared *final*.
- There is no escape of *this* from the constructor.

Contrary to Java, Python provides slightly less language directives (e.g., no final) to ensure immutability of an object. As an example, the majority of data structures (e.g., *list* and *dict*) and programmer-defined types tend to be mutable. I say the majority because exceptions exist, such as *tuples* which are immutable. Scalar types (e.g., *int, float, string*) are almost always immutable.

It is also worth to notice that the fact that an object is immutable does not mean that the *reference* is immutable.

Stateless objects are—of course—thread safe.

ACID Transactions

One way of managing concurrency is by means of ACID transactions. ACID transactions are operations such that atomicity, consistency, isolation, and durability are ensured.

Atomicity

Thread safety and atomicity are not the same thing. Indeed, thread safety is reached by means of atomicity. But atomicity is not enough to ensure thread safety.

An atomic operation is an operation that can't be broken down into multiple pieces, and that—as a consequence—is always executed as a single step.

However, if single operations are atomic, it does not imply that if multiple of them are grouped together into a single invariant (i.e., they are not independent anymore), the program stays race condition-free.

As previously said, locking mechanisms need to be used in such cases. The usage of locks ensures that the entire sequence of operations is executed successfully as a single one, or the entire work is rolled back.

Consistency

Consistency ensures that each operation starts from a valid state and after its execution, the system is in a valid state as well. Transactions are often associated with ATM operations, and it is really easy to think about consistency in this context. Missed consistency means that you go for withdrawing funds from the ATM and you do not receive money back while your account is debited with the amount of the operation. Not nice, isn't it?

Isolation

Isolation is related to the visibility of transactions. This property ensures that the output of a transaction is not visible to other transactions before it successfully completes. In other words, concurrent operations can be seen as a sequential flow of execution. Back to our banking example. If isolation is not ensured, ideally two separate bank transfers from a single account can look at the same amount of money on the account and concurrently perform the transfer. This would end up in wrong balance.

Durability

Durability means that a transaction performed on the system must persist over time. It must persist in case of crashes, in case of errors, and even in case of a zombie apocalypse if that happens.

Parallelism and Performances

When we analyze a software component, we generally consider correctness and performances.

Correctness is often inspected by means of testing and in case of concurrent programming by ensuring safety and liveness.

Guidelines on Parallel Programming

Parallel programming is generally used to improve the performances of software applications.

■ **Note**   Not all the applications can be easily parallelized.

Several trade-offs need to be made in order to ensure that parallelized code actually runs faster than its single-application variant, including, but not limited to

- Amount of parallelizable computation
- Task and data granularity
- Locality
- Load balancing

Parallelizable Computation

As we anticipated, not all the computation can actually run in parallel. Generally speaking, the nature of the problem (and data) we try to parallelize has a big impact on constraints and limitation to a successful split of simultaneous work that can be performed.

Let's consider the problem of counting the occurrences of a specific word in a document. Assume we have four servers available for computation. This problem can be easily parallelized such that

- Data is split in a uniform manner across the servers.

- Each server counts the occurrence of the given word in its portion of the document.

- When counting has been performed by all the server, relative results are summed up to obtain the entire occurrence count.

Examples like these are generally referred to as *embarrassingly parallel* problems.

Other problems, instead, are inherently sequential and notoriously known for the difficulty of trying to parallelize them. A common example in cryptography is the parallelization of hashing algorithms.

Before embarking on the parallelization journey, check if you are dealing with a problem which is notoriously known to be hard to parallelize.

Task and Data Granularity

While the nature of the problem poses impediments on whether parallelization can be performed or not, task and data granularity impact its effectiveness.

Parallelizing code comes with a cost deriving from

- Computation needed before performing the split
- The split of data and tasks across computational resources and any relevant communication required
- Idle times
- The cost adding multiple layers of abstractions or usage of frameworks to tap into parallelization capabilities

Back to our example of word counting. It is pretty intuitive that computation alone is fairly simple; however, whether parallelization is beneficial or not really depends on the size of the data and how big the chunks of data each server tackles.

The main takeaway is to always consider the size of the data, the complexity of the computation that needs to be performed, as well as scalability requirements to understand if parallelizing your application is a burden or an improvement of performances.

Locality

We experience locality of information every day: it is applied to our computers by means of hierarchical memory systems (RAM, caches, etc.). The underlying idea is that the closer the data is, the faster it is to perform computation on it.

How data is accessed also depends on the nature of the problem and data is used and reused. Specifically, always consider

- Whether or not a portion of data needs to be shared across multiple computational units

- What amount of data can be made local (close) to each computational unit

- If and which portion of data needs to be transferred from one unit to another

All these elements are fundamental to ensure that parallelization is appropriately implemented and if possible understand if and how a parallelized problem can be optimized.

Load Balancing

Back to our example of word counting and its simple solution. We inherently added the usage of a load balancer. Indeed, we considered that "data is split in a uniform manner across the servers."

Ensuring that the workload is split in a uniform manner is fundamental, yet not always a trivial task.

Load balancers add an extra layer of complexity and, hence, a potential slowdown of our application. Since they can constitute a bottleneck, carefully monitoring health and performances of a load balancer is fundamental to maintain high performances of a parallelized application.

Measuring Performances

Defining how well a parallel program is performing is a non-obvious task. It depends on multiple factors including

- How data is sent across the network
- If and how data is stored on disk
- The amount of data transmitted

Common metrics to measure performance are

- Throughput
- Latency
- Memory requirements
- Portability

Each of them needs to be prioritized, as we already said, based on the nature of problem that needs to be solved.

Anyway, two aspects which are extremely important when evaluating the performances of a distributed algorithm are

- Execution time
- Scalability

Amdahl's Law

Here is where the fun starts. Ideally, by adding resources—from one processor to multiple processors, multiple computers, or a *grid* of them—performances *"should"* linearly increase. In other words, going from a single computational resource to *n* resources, our code should run *n* times faster.

In reality, it never happens because of a sequential part always happening. In these cases, **Amdahl's law** gives a formula in order to theoretically measure the **speedup** introduced by parallelization.

The speedup *S* of a task is the ratio between the time it takes for a single processor to perform and the time it takes for multiple processors to execute the same task:

$$S = \frac{1}{1 - p + \dfrac{p}{n}}$$

The preceding formula is the speedup definition, where p is the part of the task that can be parallelized.

Observation

One of the simple, while not simplistic, ways to capture (measure) performances is by measuring the speedup introduced by parallelization via observation. Running the parallel code and running it once is not enough to have a solid idea on how the code actually performs.

Different variables should be considered and tested, including

- The number of processors
- The size of the given problem

Asymptotic Analysis

A common way to measure algorithms' performances is by means of asymptotic analysis. When using such type of analysis, performances are described as a limiting runtime behavior.

For a generic function $f(n)$, the analysis considers what happens when n becomes very large (i.e., $n \to \infty$).

As a practical example, if

$$f(n) = n^2 + constant$$

as n grows, the *constant* becomes insignificant; thus, $f(n) \sim n^2$.

And $f(n)$ is asymptotically equivalent to n^2.

Even if it is commonly accepted to describe the efficiency of an algorithm, it could not appropriately represent the performance of a parallel algorithm.

To better understand why this happens, let's consider the following runtimes in *big O* notation: $O(n)$ and $O(n \log \log n)$. Normally, $O(n \log \log n)$ grows faster than $O(n)$, thus resulting in a less efficient algorithm.

However, let's consider:

$$O(n \log \log n) = 10n + n \log \log n$$

for a parallel algorithm. For $n < 1023$, $10 n > n \log \log n$ should be considered for actual algorithm performances (not insignificant).

The key takeaway here is that, different from sequential applications, parallelized code needs extra care when analyzing real performances.

Summary

Given the complexity and broadness of the topic, in this chapter, we focused on explaining what to look at during design and review together with the relative why, rather than dealing with language-specific code how-tos. Indeed, we provided the foundation of concurrency and shown main problems to consider, including

- The need for ensuring correctness and safety of concurrent applications

- Common issues including deadlocks

- Techniques like using ACID transactions for concurrent applications

Furthermore, we touched base with basic concepts about parallelization and fundamental techniques that can be used to measure performances.

This chapter is meant to give you enough guidance for the purpose of reviews. However, if you want to learn more about how to write Python concurrent and parallel code, please refer to the *"Further Reading"* section.

In the next chapter, we will introduce the secure software development lifecycle (SSDL) and guiding principles to look at during reviews.

Further Reading

This chapter only scratches the surface of a more complex and broad area. To learn further—from basics to advanced concepts—I suggest starting with *The Art of Multiprocessor Programming* by Maurice Herlihy and Nir Shavit (Morgan Kaufmann, 2011). A more hands-on approach on how to implement high-performing code and some of the tools that are available for Python programs can be found in *High Performance Python: Practical Performant Programming for Humans* by Micha Gorelick and Ian Ozsvald (O'Reilly Media, 2nd edition, 2020).

To learn more about implementing concurrency in Python, an always green reference is Python's documentation (https://docs.python.org/3/library/concurrency.html).

Review Checklist

1. Is the code thread safe?

2. Are immutable object actually immutable?

3. Are race conditions present?

4. Is atomicity ensured?

5. Are safety and liveness ensured?

6. Are deadlocks avoided?

7. Is starvation avoided?

8. Is fairness ensured?

9. Are locking mechanisms properly used?

10. Is consistency ensured?

11. Is isolation ensured?

12. Is durability guaranteed?

13. Are you trying to parallelize a problem which is notoriously known as hard to parallelize?

14. Are you considering task and data granularity when parallelizing code?

15. Are you considering and properly embracing locality needs in your parallelized solution?

16. Is load balancing appropriately used? Is the workload uniformly split?

17. Are you considering the inherent costs of parallelizing a solution into the overall performances?

18. Do you have proper prioritization of performance metrics that are specific to the context your parallel application runs in?

Security

> I never make exceptions. An exception disproves the rule.
>
> —Sherlock Holmes in Sir Arthur Conan Doyle's
> "The Sign of Four" (1890)

First things first:

100% secure and reliable code is a unicorn.

I've been studying secure unicorns and their habits for a pretty long time. During that time, and as a conclusion of my extensive effort, I figured out that a big part of them are known as procrastinating unicorns whose famous motto is

I'll think about security later.

In other words, achieving 100% secure code is wanted by everyone, but unfeasible. Every year thousands of vulnerabilities are discovered,[1] and the exposure surface is always increasing. Although ensuring secure code also requires proper scans, especially for third-party libraries and the software we use on our infrastructure, at least the basic security principles should not be an afterthought: they need to be an integral part of any development process.

---

[1]NVD - National Vulnerability Database - statistics https://nvd.nist.gov/vuln/search/statistics?form_type=Basic&results_type=statistics&search_type=all

© Giuliana Carullo 2020
G. Carullo, *Implementing Effective Code Reviews*,
https://doi.org/10.1007/978-1-4842-6162-0_10

That being said, before dealing with what to check during a code review process, in this chapter, we will cover the security definitions and fundamentals that will walk you through the understanding of basic aspects to look for during a review.

Security Definitions

Figure 10-1 shows some of the main common terms used in the information security world.

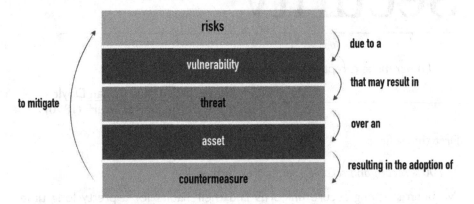

Figure 10-1. Security definitions

An **asset** is anything that is valuable for the organization, its business operations, and their continuity, including information resources that support the organization's mission.[2]

A **risk** in the general meaning provided in the project management context is an uncertain event or condition that, if it occurs, may have a positive or negative effect on one or more objectives. It may have one or more causes and it may impact one or more assets. In the context of information security, however, it only refers to negative impacts and it expresses the potential and the relative likelihood that something bad might happen.

Vulnerability and risk can be confused and used with the same meaning. However, the risk is linked to the potential of something bad happening, while the vulnerability is the channel that can be exploited to make the risk real. In other words, a vulnerability is the concrete defect that can be exploited. Vulnerabilities may be related to

---

[2]British Standard Institute, I. t. (2004). Security techniques, Management of information and communications technology security, Part 1: Concepts and models for information and communications technology security management BS ISO/IEC 13335-1-2004.

- **Software**: A security bug in a piece of software is a vulnerability.

- **Hardware**: In the physical security context, not properly enforcing restricted access to a server room is considered a vulnerability.

- **Human behavior**: Plenty of attacks exist to, for example, gain access to, otherwise confidential, information by exploiting psychological vulnerabilities.

Existing vulnerabilities expose the organization to potential damages.

The possible danger arising from the exploitation of a vulnerability that may result in harm to a system and an organization is called a **threat**. A threat may be **accidental** or **intentional** including

- Physical damages to facilities like in the case of natural events (e.g., seismic), information being compromised due to eavesdropping and theft—just to name a few.

- Accidental disclosure of confidential information by a personnel member (e.g., social engineering)

The entity that tries to exploit a vulnerability is usually referred to as a **threat agent**. The way a system gets compromised is referred to as an exploit.

To mitigate the likelihood of a risk becoming a reality, the organization identifies and put in place **countermeasures**. Back to our case of a natural disaster happening. A commonly adopted countermeasure is to consider redundancy of data and services across several geographically separated regions. Other examples of countermeasures are encryption, firewalls, security fences, access control mechanisms, and so on.

Security Is Such a PAIN

If you ask two different security people to define information security, they will probably come to you with slightly different answers. This is because security is a very broad and complex area. Anyway, all of them have three universal pillars in common: confidentiality, integrity, and availability. These three properties shown in Figure 10-2 are also commonly known as *CIA triad* and are typically used to identify weaknesses and to establish security solutions.

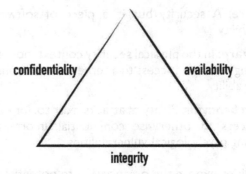

Figure 10-2. CIA triad

Confidentiality

Confidentiality ensures that only the subjects authorized to access to and use the contents of a message, a transaction, or any other data stored in the system have access to those contents. In other words, confidentiality is closely linked to privacy.

This is, for example, the case of any mailing service you use: the emails you receive need to be visible only to you, the receiver.

Some of the threats to the confidentiality of an information system are due to, for example, intruders, malware, or social engineering attacks.

To keep data and its existence secret is a problem that many organizations face, and they put a significant amount of time and money into it. This is because unauthorized access to confidential data could have a severe impact on the business, not only for critical applications. To this end, it is important to identify and classify data based on the required confidentiality in order to ensure that top priority security assets are adequately protected over time.

■ **Security by Obscurity**   Back in the day, people believed that hiding information was enough to consider it confidential. Since the beginning of mathematically sound solutions (given the time period and the technological advances), we finally stepped away from relying on obscurity to keep information secure in most cases. A very well-known practice is given by Kerckhoff's principle that states that the security of a cryptographic system should not rely on the secrecy of the algorithm, while only keys should remain secret. Since then, security by obscurity is no longer considered a secure enough practice.

Even if different security mechanisms can provide different degrees of confidentiality (availability and integrity), the main prerequisite is to protect confidentiality via cryptography, by encrypting data both *at rest* and *in transit* (i.e., moving from one system to another), and access control mechanisms. These activities need to be tracked, audited, and monitored over time.

Integrity

Integrity ensures a message, data, or transaction has not been tampered (i.e., compromised). It encompasses different properties of stored or information including correctness, completeness, consistency, and accuracy. When a security mechanism provides integrity, it prevents improper or unauthorized access and modification of data, or a resource, in a system.

An example of integrity is the case of the balance of your bank account. At any point in time, the balance needs to be correct by means of any transactions (e.g., withdraw and deposit) you legitimately performed.

Maintaining integrity also ensures that any piece of information is internally and externally consistent.

Availability

Availability ensures that information is constantly and readily accessible by authorized users. Protection mechanisms must be in place to protect against both outside and inside threats that could affect the availability of the organization's assets.

Back to our bank account example. Ensuring availability means that accessing the various banking services should work anytime you need to.

■ **Facts from the World** Availability is generally formalized contractually by means of SLA (service-level agreements). Critical services, like those provided in the telecommunication world, generally strive for at least five-nine availability. This means that services should be available 99.999% of the time. In such a case, the maximum allowed downtime of a service is less than 5 minutes and 26 seconds in every given year.

Typical attacks against availability are denial of service (DoS) attacks and its distributed form DDoS. Anyhow, when dealing with system availability, it should also be taken into account possible power outages as well as risks due to natural disasters (i.e., physical security). Between all, properly implementing redundancy is the very first step into achieving availability.

Non-repudiation

The CIA triad is sometimes also referred to as PAIN, which stands for privacy, availability/authentication, integrity, and non-repudiation.

Non-repudiation means that an action cannot be denied. Any action (e.g., access or modification) is bounded to a unique subject. For instance, this property ensures that after a message is sent, it cannot be disputed if it has been sent or not.

Back to our email example; this means that if a friend sends you an email, they cannot argue whether they sent it or not.

Trade-offs

Implementing the right controls, based on security requirements, is fairly intricate. Trade-offs are made all the time between the various triad aspects. Certain aspects might require priority, but a balance should always be considered. Consider, for example, a scenario where high confidentiality is highly enforced but availability is neglected: in case of an attack, even the subject with the right permission would not be able to access anything.

Back to our banking example, high confidentiality means that the account holder is the only person allowed to access banking services. However, a lack of availability implies that not even the account holder can use services even if they should be allowed to.

Not balancing properly security requirements given the criticality of the offered services, the environment they run into, as well as any legal obligation would cost a lot for the industry, both in terms of money and reputation.

Fact or Fiction?

The adage "think first, then act" applies to coding as well as security. The "think first" is also known as *security by design*, which means that the software is born as secure. It is designed from the ground up to be secure. Secure is how software is meant to be.

Unfortunately, too often new solutions are built and delivered without dealing with security and privacy issues from time zero. Only later, maybe when some attacks and relative money losses took place, people think how to make their product secure and compliant.

Too many times securing a software seems like distracting from the final goal: releasing the product. Securing any piece of code surely comes with some costs. However, trying to secure an unsecured solution later on during its lifetime is not going to be a viable solution because think about it

1. The business who releases insecure software loses in credibility.

2. The business loses money.

3. It is so much more difficult to add security features later on in the software lifecycle.

4. It is costlier and more time consuming to fix after rather than designing first.

It is like you cooked brownies, but you forgot to add chocolate before baking them, right? It is a huge no, no, no!

Security Principles

Now more than ever, when tons of solutions are deployed into the Cloud and we are (almost) all excited by the Internet of Things wave, using the security by design model is mandatory. And, surely, the underlying principles described as follows can be used to assess code during reviews.[3]

Least Privilege

Least privilege states that any subject should be given the minimum possible privilege on the minimum portion of resources for the minimum amount of time (Figure 10-3). In other words, a user should be given only those privileges which are strictly required to perform its designated task.

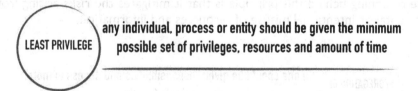

LEAST PRIVILEGE — any individual, process or entity should be given the minimum possible set of privileges, resources and amount of time

Figure 10-3. Least privilege

---

[3]OWASP Developer Guide, www.owasp.org/index.php/Developer_Guide

A simple example application is often enforced in physical security: you do not have access to an office unless you need to (e.g., you work for the company who owns/rents that specific office).

Defense in Depth

Defense in depth is about providing multilayer protection: subsequent layer will provide protection if a previous one is breached (Figure 10-4). The reasoning behind this principle is that combining several layers of different types of security mechanisms is the only way to deploy a reasonably secure environment: attackers would need to overcome all the levels of protection that surround the protected assets in order to gain access to it.

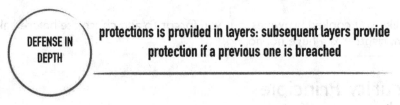

Figure 10-4. Defense in depth

As an an example, think about a simple multilayered software consisting of an API, some backend computation, and a database. Attempting to secure only the API is insufficient: any circumvention of the API would leave backend and data exposed to possible attacks.

Segregation of Duties

The *segregation of duties* (SoD) principle states that no person should be given responsibility or access to more than one related function (Figure 10-5). The reasoning behind this principle is that it mitigates the risks arising from accidental or intentional misuse of resources and information.

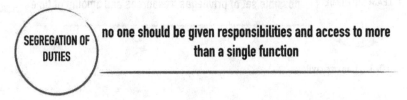

Figure 10-5. Segregation of duties

This is as simple as thinking about the development tools we use every day, *git* included. Segregation of duties happens when you are granted read/write permissions to the projects your team owns, but you do not have permissions, by default, to the other projects within the company.

Fail Safe

The *fail safe* principle states that if a system fails, it should fail to a state in which security and data are not compromised (Figure 10-6). It means that the default access rights for any entity to any resource is no access.

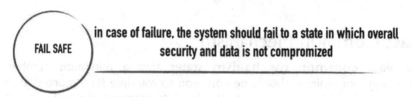

Figure 10-6. Fail safe

Let's consider the case of a database. Fail safe, applied to transactions performed on a database, means that if, for example, a write happens to be unsuccessful midway before it is fully performed, the safe state would be

1. No data actually changed.

2. Error is signaled and handled accordingly.

Back to our banking system. If you attempt to perform a withdrawal, but no money can be released by the ATM, fail safe means that the error is clear and the failure of the withdrawal is reflected by no change into the balance of your checking account.

Complete Mediation

Complete mediation means that every request by a subject to access an object must be authorized, without exceptions (Figure 10-7). Indeed, it applies to every protected or unprotected object in the system. This principle imposes the constraint of identifying every subject attempting to access an object. Thus, it enables a consistent access control of the whole system, thus improving security as well as assurance and confidence.

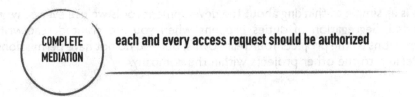

each and every access request should be authorized

Figure 10-7. Complete mediation

As an example, complete mediation means that you won't access to any of the data and services (either critical or not) on your laptop unless you authenticated yourself and authorization has been granted.

Least Common Mechanism

The **least common mechanism** states that a minimum number of protection mechanisms should be common to multiple (i.e., more than one) users, since shared access paths may lead to information leakage (Figure 10-8). In other words, mechanisms to access resources should not be shared.

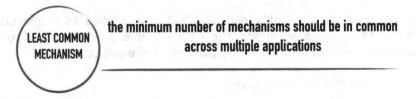

the minimum number of mechanisms should be in common across multiple applications

Figure 10-8. Least common mechanism

Consider, for example, two virtual machines, each running a service with a different set of users. Those two virtual machines need to be properly isolated in order to guarantee no leakage from one machine to another.

Weakest Link

The **weakest link** principle stresses how important it is to identify—and mitigate—the weakest mechanisms in the security chain and layers of defense (Figure 10-9).

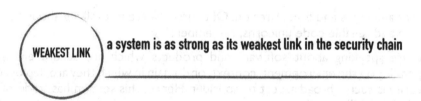

WEAKEST LINK a system is as strong as its weakest link in the security chain

Figure 10-9. Weakest link

Generally speaking, the commonly known weakest link is ourselves as humans and the usage we do of a system. Phishing and social engineering attacks are at the order of the day, and there is not much security a system can offer if we willingly, yet unconsciously, volunteer information.

Security Principles Caveats

The described principles do not look like rocket science. However, they are a huge boost in securing any solution. Bad things always happen (*Murphy's law*), but I think that—really—starting from the foundations of security principles and software development is the way to go. It does not end there for sure, but they are still underrated nowadays.

Worth noting, however, that any of these fundamental principles can be very complex depending on the technologies used and the context they run into.

As an example, let's go back to the least common mechanism: isolating virtual machines is not the same as isolating containers that, in turn, is not the same as separating flows within a given service on top of them depending on the specific business logic and usage expectations.

Security Code Review

I strongly suggest to have broader security-specific reviews including

- Security implication of the used programming language
- Automation and penetration testing
- Security architecture reviews
- Broad checks of the security of third-party libraries the code depends on.

However, some checks can and need to be performed during the development process, even for not-so-mature software. I can't stress enough how thinking about security earlier in the process can save you from a lot of headaches, as well as and costs and time, later on. Of course we are not talking about 100% secure and reliable code unicorns, remember?

We are speaking about software and products which are secure enough depending on the environment, context, or domain in which they are deployed. Security is such a broad aspect to consider. Hence, this section has trade-offs in mind and will walk through some of the main aspects to look at during code reviews to ensure that at least major flaws are checked.

Secure Software Development Lifecycle

Security code reviews are only a small piece into the secure software development lifecycle (SSDLC).

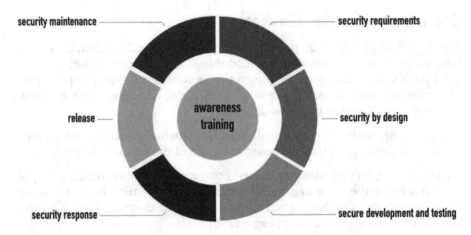

Figure 10-10. Secure software development lifecycle (SSDLC)

As anticipated, security should be by design. However, there is much more that goes into a proper SSDLC (Figure 10-10). Specifically

- Security is a critical piece of any software application and a very complex one. Proper awareness training on the topic is fundamental to the security process and is generally provided by most companies.

- As we saw, a good understanding of context and environment in which the application operates is fundamental to understand security requirements, implications, and potential risks from the get-go.

- Always consider security by design.

- Secure development and testing (reviews performed here as detailed in the following section).

- It is very important to have an outlined security/incident response plan in place ahead of releasing the code. In other words, it is fundamental to have and know which processes are in place in case an incident happens and who is supposed to resolve it within which time frame.

- Depending whether code needs to be publicly released or not, extra processes (company specific) are generally in place.

- Last, but not least, like general code quality, it is important to consider how to maintain security over time.

Facts from the World Companies, especially in heavily regulated environments like healthcare, need to go through *auditing* processes of their systems to ensure compliance against a multitude of legal regulations that depend on both the sector they work in and their geographical location. We will not provide details about auditing processes in this book since they are generally broader and way more complex than day-to-day software development process for most engineers.

Security Code Reviews

A security code review serves the purpose of ensuring that major inconsistencies and other flows, not already detected, are still looked at. Figure 10-11 shows the software development lifecycle (SDLC) and highlights in which phase security code reviews are usually performed.

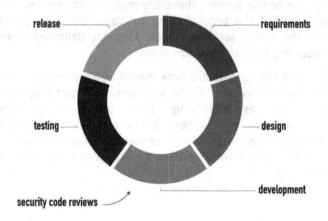

Figure 10-11. Security code review

Generally speaking, such reviews focus on finding exposure to potential threats in the areas discussed earlier, that is, availability, confidentiality, and integrity. However, those are pretty broad, since they span across checking for identity and access management, how sessions are managed, data privacy, logging, error handling, confidential information, and encryption, just to mention some.

Automating Security Reviews

Automated code reviews might help a lot in speeding up the review—we love automation, don't we?

Static application security testing (SAST) tools can be used to support static code analysis and help find security flaws. Generally speaking, they are very useful during the development process, and they are fairly easy to embed during the development phase.

As an example, GitLab CI/CD offers easy integration with SAST (https://docs.gitlab.com/ee/user/application_security/sast/) and can be used to spot both the existence unsafe code that could potentially be used for unintended code execution and XSS attacks.

■ **Note** Plenty of SAST tools exist that can be used depending on the language, your programming environment and preferences. OWASP (https://owasp.org/www-community/Source_Code_Analysis_Tools) provides a fairly comprehensive list of options. Consider adding a SAST tool to your SSDLC.

At the other side of the seesaw, there are manual code reviews that require a good knowledge of the programming language, domain, application, use cases, and—in this case—security as well. They are definitely more complex and time consuming than using automation.

However, some of the aspects like how identities are managed can be better detected via manual reviews. Code scanners can speed up the process, especially if the code base is fairly big. Their use is useful especially as a first pass. Anyway, they may lack context, hence possibly producing both false positives and false negatives. Thus, I encourage you to automatize when possible but still embed manual reviews to ensure as much as possible code quality and security.

Summary

Security code reviews help in finding flaws in the code. But don't be fooled. You will not spot all of them. Remember that having healthy code is about constant improvements. With security, it is also about constant monitoring. Certain issues are not that easy to detect and code reviews per se surely will not solve them. Monitor data based on the context of your application to discover anomalous behaviors, and if that happens, start to find the root cause.

Especially for security, there is no one size fits them all.

Key takeaways

- Always consider security by design.

- Consider the trade-offs and any consequent risk of the software you write.

- Always consider at least the security implications given by the fundamental principles described in this chapter.

- Have both manual and automatized reviews and processes in place.

In the next chapter, we will put together the entire code review process and provide guidance on metrics to track and monitor during the review process. Furthermore, we will depict common behavioral issues that can make or break its effectiveness.

Further Reading

Security can't really be condensed in a couple of readings. To inspect deeper on the foundation of security, the *Official (ISC) 2 Guide to the CISSP CBK, 3rd ed.* by Steven Hernandez (Auerbach Publications, 2012) is surely not a lightweight read, while an amazing reference. OWASP (https://owasp.org/) also provides a nice guidance on application security.

Review Checklist

Some of the following questions might be excluded depending on the type of software you might be dealing with, but they are meant to be as general as possible to be a good guidance during the review process.

1. Is any sensitive/private/confidential information logged?

2. Is any sensitive/private/confidential information disclosed?

3. Are audit trails present?

4. Are authentication and authorization mechanisms consistently enforced? Are they adequate to the intended security degree wanted?

5. Is every access to an object authorized (i.e., complete mediation)?

6. Is the least privilege principle enforced?

7. Is defense in depth applied?

8. Is segregation of duties principle ensured?

9. In case of failures, does the system fail safely?

10. Is encryption performed? Is it adequate to the security needs?

11. Are weak ciphers used?

12. Are security keys too small to provide adequate security?

13. Are certificates valid?

14. Are security keys protected from unauthorized access?

15. Are hashing mechanisms used to check for integrity when needed?

16. Are security tests in place?

17. Which is the weakest link in the security chain? Is it secure enough?

18. Are systems secure enough to expose the least attack surface as possible?

19. Are all entry points to the system secured?

20. Is input validated against well-known attacks (e.g., SQL injection, XSS injection)?

21. Does the system plan for failure?

22. Is security by obscurity in place instead of proper mechanisms?

23. Does the code contain any security bug (also language dependent)?

24. Are privacy-enhanced protocols in place when required?

25. Are the used protocols tamper resistant?

26. Is the code resistant to buffer overflow?

27. Is there any hard-coded password?

28. Is there any backdoor in the code?

29. Is the code compliant with security policies and standards?

30. Are security requirements clear?

31. Is the team well trained on security?

32. Are security response plan and processes in place?

Code Reviews

Nothing clears up a case so much as stating it to another person.

—Sherlock Holmes in Sir Arthur Conan Doyle's
"The Adventure of Silver Blaze" (1892)

We covered so far a fairly large spectrum of good practices and checks to perform to ensure quality of our software.

This last chapter focuses on the process itself, highlighting

- Clean code lifecycle
- Metrics
- Collaboration challenges
- How to spot flaws in the code without making programmers feel bad
- Recommendations for managers

Wrapping Up

Before we get into metrics and final recommendations, let's wrap up what we've covered in this book and see how it all fits together with the clean code lifecycle (CCLC) (Figure 11-1).

© Giuliana Carullo 2020
G. Carullo, *Implementing Effective Code Reviews*,
https://doi.org/10.1007/978-1-4842-6162-0_11

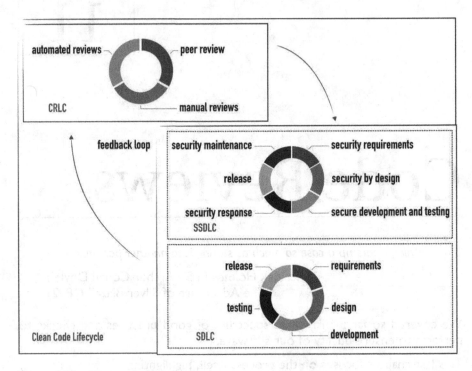

Figure 11-1. Clean code lifecycle

Adding a variety of code reviews can feel complex and burdensome. But it does need to be. At the end of the day, both classical SDLC and SSDLC should go hand in hand as shown in Figure 11-1. To perform code reviews at their best, we need a well-rounded code review lifecycle (CRLC) that is comprised of

- **Peer reviews**: Generally performed during development phase

- **Automation**: When feasible

- **Regular comprehensive manual reviews**

By considering the feedback loop between the lifecycles, we can ensure and maintain clean and secure code over time.

Next, we will provide metrics on how to perform better informed decisions on the feedback and gather insights on how successfully our code is moving toward a better version of itself.

Code Metrics

Some metrics can be used to gather a high-level view of the code base status, including

- Defect density
- Defect removal effectiveness

Defect Density

Defect density (DD) describes the number of faults occurred per *lines of code (LOCs)*. It can be used to have a really high-level view of the status of the code base.

$$DD = \frac{defects\ found}{LOCs}$$

Indeed, as we early described in this book, just counting defects is not enough, and each of them should be properly prioritized.

As an example, consider the case of a security code review, where different vulnerabilities might be discovered. Not all of them are created equal. Nor their impact to the business. In this case, defect density would give a *quantitative* view, not a *qualitative* view.

Defect Removal Effectiveness

Defect removal effectiveness (DRE), also referred to as **defect removal efficiency**, expresses a measure of effectiveness of solving issues during the software lifecycle.

It is generally useful to determine product's healthiness and can be applied to code review. DRE can be defined in terms of reviews as follows:

$$DRE = \frac{defects\ found\ or\ removed}{defects\ latent\ or\ introduced\ in\ the\ code}\ (100\%)$$

Defects Found

Table 11-1 shows a sample table template that wraps together the entire review process we analyzed so far and that helps in summarizing the number of defects found during code reviews.

Table II-I. Sample Table—Tracking Defects Found

Stage	Description	Defects Found
Functional	Bugs found during review	5
Code smells	Code smells described in the book	100
Design	Design issues discovered during review	10
Requirements	Defects in functional and/or nonfunctional requirements	3
Architecture	Architectural defects	8
Overall health	Including human resources and processes	0
Security	Security flaws detected	3

Defects Latent

Defects found are helpful when a single code review is performed. However, defects latent (i.e., unfixed defects) and newly introduced ones are really important to track over time to ensure that the code is actually improving and that the work required is sustainable.

However, these defects can be harder to calculate or estimate.

In case of incremental code reviews (i.e., another review has already been performed), previous number of defects found can be considered. If the number of defects found with a later review is bigger than the previous one, it might signal that new defects were actually introduced in the code.

This is not 100% accurate, of course, in terms of granularity of the defects' type. Nonetheless, it provides a broad indicator of health status of the code.

Other types of estimation can be performed (e.g., industry experience), but, analogously, they might result in not too accurate defects count.

Review Metrics

Other than the code per se, we also want to evaluate our processes. Thus, in this section, we are going to uncover metrics that we can use to have a better understanding of how effective the code review process is. Specifically we will look at

- Inspection rate (IR)
- Code coverage (CC)
- Defect detection rate (DDR)

Inspection Rate

Inspection rate (IR) gives insights on the velocity of the review process. Indeed it is defined as

$$IR = \frac{LOCs}{hours}$$

where *LOCs* is the number of lines of code of the analyzed component and *hours* is the amount of hours spent in performing the review.

This metrics is oftentimes used to get an understanding of the quality of the performed review. A lot of opinions have been expressed about a guess of which IR values express a well-performed review.

I personally do not buy into it as it is and I would still contextualize this type of information and perform an educated validation.

The IR might be impacted by many factors, including

- The current code quality
- The experience of the reviewer
- The number of feedbacks left as regards defects found
- The quality of these feedbacks
- Whether or not the reviewer is already familiar with the architecture and code

Code Coverage

Code coverage is the degree of code being inspected. In code reviews, the expected coverage is 100%.

But remember: always break down complex tasks into smaller, more manageable problems. It's true that complete code reviews should be regularly included into the development process. However, better to start reviewing code as soon as possible after a change is performed or a new feature is added to the codebase (e.g., peer reviews). It will make things easier when the complete review will be due and it will help in achieving better code on the go.

Defect Detection Rate

Defect detection rate (DDR) expresses the velocity of finding defects. It is computed as

$$DDR = \frac{defects\ found}{hours}$$

The approach for looking at this metric is equivalent to the one used for inspection rate. Use it, but do it with caution and evaluate it depending on the context. Certain times code is so bad that defects jump out from everywhere, other times it is already in a fairly good shape (in which case, high five!).

Recommendations and Guidelines

Let's wrap the review process with some overarching guidelines on it.

Clear Review Goals

It is important to clarify what the objectives of the review are. This will help you to be on track during the process. The objectives will depend, between all, on environment, stage of the project, requirements, scope, and technologies used.

Stay Scientific, Stay SMART

Avoid recommendations like "a faster DB/component/similar would be cool." Argue what is actually needed (measurable), why, and the impact on the project.

Use the SMART approach. Always be specific with the defects, and have measurable and achievable suggested improvements. Reviews insights should be relevant to both the type of review you are performing and the problem to be solved. And they should be time bounded by means of having specific actions to be taken to remove defects with a specific deadline.

Example of a bad feedback is

> There are too many dependencies between Component 1 and Component 2. This is due to bad design. Change it.

A better form would be

There are a lot of dependencies between Component 1 and Component 2 due to design smell X. The design can be improved by refactoring and by applying the design pattern Y. This is an important defect; consider fixing it in the next couple of Sprints.

■ **Refresher**   In Scrum methodology, a Sprint is a time box, generally one month or less, during which a Sprint goal is achieved. The outcome of the Sprint is a potentially releasable to production increment of work.

Plan Ahead

Have a plan on what to fix. Always set up priorities to address defects based on their urgency. Suggestions on possible ways to fix them are very welcome. Consider tracking defects using the template table shown in Table 11-2. The template is meant to track improvements needed in a SMART way.

Table 11-2. Tracking Defects: Sample Template

No.	Defect	Type	Component	Priority	Suggestion
1	What the defect is	Defect type	Component in the code that suffers from the defect	High/medium/low	Suggestion for improvement specific to the code

An example of application of the template is given in Table 11-3.

Table 11-3. Tracking Defects: Sample Table

No.	Defect	Type	Component	Priority	Suggestion
1	Feature density	Design smell	MyComponent.py	High	MyComponent breaks the single responsibility principle and implements two separate independent behaviors. Specifically it should be broken down into Component1 and Component2

■ **Note**   Especially if you are using Agile methodologies, filling in tables can be an extra burden. They key point of having a table is to track reviews and changes needed. However, this information can be tracked in any other shape or form depending on the development process in place. As an example, if you are working with Scrum, consider ticketing accordingly instead of filling in a table and discuss findings during planning sessions.

Checklists Are Simply Not Enough

Checklists are very useful as guidance during reviews. However, just walking through a checklist is not enough, and other methods, including scenario-based architecture reviews, should be considered. This would enable a well-rounded assessment.

Code Reviews for Developers

There are as many ways to perform bad code reviews as writing bad software. Code reviews can be really helpful if done right and a waste of time if done wrong.

That's a Trap

Possible issues can fall into three broad categories:

- Allowing the review to be judgmental
- Making the review personal
- Becoming frustrated with a tedious review process

One of the biggest traps that threaten code reviews is the risk of allowing the process to become *judgmental*. This approach toward code reviews creates a toxic work environment, destroys team morale, and hinders the production process.

Please, avoid approaching reviews as a way to challenge colleagues. Easier said than done, I get you. Hone your communication skills, if you have to. Almost everybody has rolled their eyes while looking at some not-that-cool code before, but resist the urge to let it cloud your review. Please, go into the process with a positive attitude: help, teach, and reward success. Don't jab your finger at other people's flaws. Constructive feedback goes a long way. Reviews can and need to be a team building activity and a learning experience.

Also competition should be avoided. Sometimes our ego can step into the game:

> *Oh Mark's code is only so-so. I could write it so much better. My code is beautiful. I'm a true pythonista, unlike Mark.*

I get it. I love beautiful code, but let's keep competition out of the door. Code reviews are not an unhealthy challenge on who writes the most beautiful code in the team.

The second trap is the risk of making the review personal. The defect is in the code; you are not scanning colleagues. The code does something in a wrong way; it is not about Mark or Mary. Thus, be careful to communicate defects in the proper way, nothing personal.

The third trap, nonetheless important, is about being frustrated with a tedious review process.

Let's consider reviews performed before each *merge* request. How many of you have been stuck waiting for a colleague to review the code? How many waited too long to perform a review?

Some don'ts are

- Do not be a perfectionist; it simply does not exist. Good code is not perfect code. Not liking a minutia in the code is not a valid option to question and/or reject the code under review.

- Do not create big branches/commits. Help your colleagues and they will help you out in turn. Keeping commits focused and short will make reviews fast enough and far more manageable.

Manners

First and foremost, if you volunteered or you have been asked to perform a code review, **commit to it**. Do it accurately, walk through all the steps, and don't just glide over it.

Hence, **do not just assume that the code works**, not because it comes from a more senior peer. Remember! We are not scanning people. You trust your colleagues for doing a great job, and that's amazing. But it does not imply that you do not have to do a great job yourself. **Rebuild and test the code**. How many of you found yourself in the situation of ending up with broken tests? Maybe because of a change in an interface? Fully commit to the process and do your best.

If the code integrates well, do not stop the process here. If a new functionality is developed, **inspect for documentation and additional tests needed**. Is the committed code accompanied by proper documentation and use cases? If not, it is the right moment to raise the necessity and fix it.

A common dispute is about deciding if code reviews include testing or not. This is especially true for teams where a defined distinction is made between who does reviews and who cares about quality assurance (QA). My thought is already clear. During code reviews, some testing needs to be done. Catching bugs and flaws is not the responsibility of a single person or team. The sooner they are detected and fixed, the better; period.

If you found the code hard to read and understand, **do not make biased decisions**. Nor the perception of your own or someone-else seniority should have any impact on the review. Do not be scared to ask the programmer who wrote the code for a clarification about the context and the approach they used to implement it. Readability is a huge principle in good code. The worst that can happen is that you learn something or something was missing and the code improves. Not that bad, isn't it?

Finally, after the review, **do not skip reviewing again**. Does the new code incorporate all the required changes? Rebuild and retest. Check again for documentation and additional tests. All of the steps should be made. Second review might be slightly faster, but cannot be taken at ease. Reviewing can be daunting, but it is worthwhile in the end.

Code Reviews for Managers

It is fair enough to address code reviews also from a manager perspective. As engineers, architects, and tester, you name it, you should have already recognized how much value this process adds to the overall code quality. Thus, this section is specifically designed for all managers.

Oftentimes, code reviews are seen as yet another costly process that distracts engineers from writing more functionalities. This demonstrates yet another conflict between quantity and quality. And if I did not convince you so far on how much they can improve the development process, please allow me to highlight how you can directly benefit from them.

Quality Means Faster

Especially in Agile teams, adding code reviews looks like a lot of effort that adds up to the already full Sprints. Sure enough quality code comes with a price. But quality code also implies a faster development process. If the code is incrementally constantly improved, developing new features is faster. With less bugs, anomalies, and with greater readability and usability, the team is allowed to focus each and every time to keep on providing value (actual functionalities) rather than being constantly stopped because of unclear, unstructured, or buggy code that needs to be fixed first.

In other words, it helps in reducing **firefighting**. Firefighting happens when different priorities take over on each other causing a lot of context changes.

As shown in Figure 11-2, when firefighting happens, the engineer needs to eventually interrupt the development process to fix the defect and test again and only after they can go back to developing the actual feature. This slows down the process and reduces productivity.

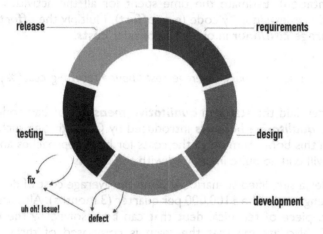

Figure 11-2. Firefighting

Distributed Teams

Any engineering manager knows how tough it can be at times to manage a team especially if it is geographically distributed. Communication is slightly more intricate than "normal" teams.

To deal with it, a lot of meetings are added to the daily work to facilitate communication. Anyway, as developers, we communicate with both verbal language and code. Thus, you should not only care that all the interacting team members share a common language (e.g., English), but they should also share the same coding process and (good) practices.

Show Me the Math

If I did not convince you so far, let's gather some numbers with a little exercise: a **cost benefit analysis (CBA)**. Code reviews can save company's money. I strongly suggest that you compile a table distinguishing between **recurring** and **non-recurring** costs for both development process with and without code reviews.

Fill up the table based on the *average cost/hour* of a team member.

For both recurring and non-recurring costs, add the various activities (e.g., issues due to bugs, time spent in troubleshooting, effort due to lack of clarity of documentation). Estimate the time spent for all the activities with and without code reviews/quality code (e.g., **effort**). Multiply the **effort in hours** and the **average cost/hour** in order to consider **costs**.

$$Costs = Effort\ in\ hours * average\ cost\ /\ hour * recurring\ cost\ (\%)$$

As a reminder, add the status in **qualitative measure** for bad code without reviews and **qualitative benefits** introduced by QA activities such as those explained in this book. Sum up all the costs for both approaches and you are done. You will end up quite impressed with the results.

Let's consider a simplified scenario. Assume the average cost of development for a single engineer to be $100,000 per quarter (3 months). Also assume that you found a piece of technical debt that can be resolved by the team in 2 weeks. Let's also assume that the team is composed of three engineers collaborating on the same codebase.

The first option would be to not fix it and keep going with new features. Table 11-4 shows a simplified set of estimates for recurring costs in such scenario.

Table 11-4. CBA: Not Fixing Technical Debt

What	Recurring Cost	Cost
Troubleshooting	10% slowdown of the entire development process	$100,000 x 3 x 10% = $30,000
Adding a new functionality in dependent software	15% slowdown of the entire development process	$100.000 x 3 x 15% = $45,000
Lack of documentation	5% slowdown of the entire development process	$100,000 x 3 x 5% = $15,000
Total		**$90,000**

The second option would be to allocate 1 month for improving the code. See Table 11-5.

Table 11-5. CBA: Fixing Technical Debt

What	Non Recurring Cost	Cost
Fixing tech debt	2 weeks cost of 3 engineers	$15,343[1] x 3 = 46,029
Total		**$46,029**

The beauty of this is that technical debt is a recurring cost. This means that not fixing it (in our example) will end up in costing $90,000 every quarter until it gets finally resolved.

Differently, not only fixing a given piece of technical debt has (in this case) a lower cost per quarter (i.e., $46,029). It saves money in the long run.

Indeed, suppose that the technical debt goes unfixed for an entire year. While fixing technical debt would stop at $46,029 in costs, the overall recurring cost for not fixing it would pile up to a grand total of $360,000 in a year. You can also quickly imagine how those numbers would snowball if we consider bigger teams and several pieces of technical debt that need to be resolved.

■ **Note** This is, as anticipated, a simplified scenario. Granularity can be modified depending on the given context at hand. Furthermore, overall, we cannot isolate technical debt from strategy and other feature commitments. The recommendation here is to plug in your numbers and estimates and check the math in your context. Math never lies.

Summary

In this chapter, we wrapped the review process by providing high-level guidance on how to approach code reviews both as an engineer and a manager, and we discussed some metrics that can help you in tracking improvements over time.

Key takeaways from this last chapter

- Gather some metrics and do not trust only your instinct about code improving or not over time.
- Soft skills are as much valued as technical ones.

---

[1]Considering 4.345 weeks in a month.

▓ **Warning** Managers love a nice work environment as much as you do. Having to call out cases of not playing as a team makes them cry. I told you.

Further Reading

Best Kept Secrets of Peer Code Review by Jason Cohen (Smart Bear, 2006) and *Peer Reviews in Software* by Karl Weigers (Addison-Wesley Professional, 2002) are interesting references on peer reviews. *Software Inspection* by Tom Gilb and Dorothy Graham (Addison-Wesley Professional, 1994) provides nice insights on the overall inspection process.

Review Checklist

In this last bit of review checklist, we are going to review how reviews are performed.

1. Do you approach the process with a positive attitude?

2. Are you nonjudgmental with colleagues?

3. Are you choosy and rejecting reviews only because of nitpicking minutia in the reviewed code?

4. Is competition out of the door?

5. Is the process tedious?

6. Are you making the defects more about the programmer rather than the code?

7. Are you rewarding success?

8. Are you valuing teaching more than critiquing?

9. Are commits gigantic scattered pieces of code that need to be reviewed?

10. Are you using code reviews as a way of improving communication within the team?

11. Are you using code reviews as a learning experience?

12. Are the objectives of the code review clearly defined?

13. Are feedbacks and recommendation stated in a SMART way?

14. Is the review followed by a plan to put in action to fix defects?

15. Are you fully committed as a reviewer?

16. Are you biased by the perception of yourself (e.g., too young or too senior to perform a review)?

17. Are you biased by the perception of others?

18. Are you glancing over code?

19. Do you rebuild and test the code?

20. Do you check that the code is accompanied by additional doc and tests?

21. If code is unclear, do you ask for clarification?

22. If you asked for a change, do you carefully review again the newer code to ensure important defects have been addressed?

23. Are all asked changes properly prioritized and addressed?

Conclusions

Always code as if the guy who ends up maintaining your code will be a violent psychopath who knows where you live.

—John F. Woods, game programmer (1991)

I hope this book has been useful for you in order to navigate the journey of good code and the process of code reviews. I also hope that coding wisdom is with you and that it will stay with you for a long time.

Learning is a continuous process. Each book is different every time we read it, because we—during our learning process—become a different person. Go back and read the book again every time a refresher is needed. Brush up on the concepts and most importantly apply them into your code.

Here are some final words of wisdom:

- First code. Then improve it. Then make it better.

- Don't be scared to make mistakes; we all do.

- Don't try to have the absolute perfect architecture and code at the very start.

- We all start prototyping—often very fast in order to quickly validate an early concept. But do not forget to go back to it.

- Improve it every time you touch the code.

And in the end, both your skills and your code will be grand!

All the best!

G. Carullo, *Implementing Effective Code Reviews*,
https://doi.org/10.1007/978-1-4842-6162-0

Glossary

Abstract factory Creational design pattern aimed at hiding complexity during object creation.

ACID Properties often used in the context of software transactions. The acronym stands for atomicity, consistency, isolation, and durability.

Adapter Structural design pattern that improves interoperability by wrapping another object, redefining its interface.

Agile Methodology used in project management and software engineering. It is based on the idea of continuous, incremental, and iterative sequences of work (namely, sprints).

Ambiguous interfaces Design smell specific to APIs. It happens when they are not clearly and well defined.

Amdahl's law Formula that defines how to theoretically measure the speedup introduced by parallelization.

API Application programming interface. It defines how communication is meant to happen between various components, systems, or objects.

Array Basic data structures that store homogeneous elements. These elements can be accessed by means of indexing.

Asset A general term used to refer to anything that is valuable for an organization.

Asymptotic analysis A mathematical approach to limit a behavior. In computer science, it is used to describe the performances of algorithms.

Atomicity In concurrent programming, atomicity refers to an operation that can't be broken down into multiple pieces and that—as a consequence—is always executed as a single step.

G. Carullo, *Implementing Effective Code Reviews*,
https://doi.org/10.1007/978-1-4842-6162-0

Availability In security, it is fundamental property of a system. It ensures that information is constantly and readily accessible by (authorized) users.

Binary search tree Data structure also known as ordered binary tree. It is a binary tree that is stored as sorted in memory in order to allow fast lookup, add, and remove operations.

Binary tree Data structure organized like a tree that enforces the following property: each node in the tree has at most two children.

Bug pollution Terms used to refer to bugs growing in size and number within in a system. This usually happens when they are not promptly addresses.

Builder Creational design pattern that simplifies the creation of a complex object by breaking down the creation into smaller separated tasks.

Chain of responsibility Behavioral design pattern used to foster decoupling the sender of request from the receiver.

CIA triad In security, a triad that describes the core security principles that needs to be considered for every system. It includes confidentiality, integrity, and availability.

Clean code lifecycle (CCLC) Lifecycle that embraces software development lifecycle (SDLC), secure software development lifecycle (SSDLC), and code review lifecycle (CRLC). It is meant to maintain clean code over time.

Code smell Term coined by Martin Fowler and Kent Beck to call out issues in the code that are indicators of deeper problems within the system.

Code reviews Technique used to systematically examine the codebase to find defects or potential flaws.

Code review lifecycle (CRLC) Lifecycle that ensures, by means of different review types, that the codebase qualitatively improves over time.

Coding conventions Guidelines that vary for each programming language. They include recommendation regarding style, indentation, comments, common practices, and so on.

Coupling The number of dependencies between classes, methods, and interfaces within the code.

Cyclic dependency Design smell also known as circular dependency. It happens when two or more components depend on each other.

Comments Human readable explanation of the purposes and inner working of the source code.

Comments-driven development (CDD) Methodology used in computer programming that is centered on writing plain text description of the code first, then the actual implementation.

Complete mediation Fundamental principle of secure systems. It states that every request by a subject to access an object in the system must be authorized, without any exceptions.

Composite Structural design pattern that aims managing a group of complex objects and single objects exposing similar functionalities in a uniform manner.

Composition In object-oriented programming, composition is a way to group simple objects into more complex ones.

Concurrency Refers to the ability of a software system to execute multiple independent pieces of computation without affecting the final result.

Confidentiality Fundamental property of a secure system. If ensured, only the subjects authorized to access to information within a system can actually do it.

Consistency In concurrent programming, consistency ensures that each operation starts from a valid state, and after its execution, the system is in a valid state as well.

Control structures In programming, it is a code block that changes the sequence of logic that a program executes at runtime.

Core The basic computational unit within a CPU.

Cost benefit analysis (CBA) Approach oftentimes used in project management to estimate the strengths and weaknesses of possible alternatives.

Countermeasure In security, a countermeasure is an action aimed at mitigating the likelihood of a potential risk becoming a reality.

CPU Central processing unit. Basic computational circuit in a computer.

Critical section In concurrent programming, it is a portion of shared code/ memory that needs to be protected by concurrent accesses in order to guarantee correctness of the system.

Critical region Alternative name for the critical section.

Data structure Collection of elements, organized according to inner rules. Depending on the internal organization, an interface is provided in order to operate on data. Common operations are access, add, remove, and search.

Deadlock In concurrent programming, a deadlock is an unwanted condition that happens if two or more processes are blocking each other. This happens if each of them is waiting for the release of a given resource from the others.

Decorator Structural design pattern that enables reusability by means of enhancing an object's behavior.

Defense in depth Fundamental principle in security. It specifies that a system must provide multilayer protection. The core idea is that if one layer is breached, the others can compensate and let the system remain secure.

Design (SDLC) Phase of the software development lifecycle that aims at defining the software architecture, together with coding guidelines, languages and tools, frameworks, and platforms.

Design document specification (DSS) Specification that documents the output of the design phase.

Design pattern Well-known solution for recurrent categories of problems within software systems.

Design smell Indicators of issues at architecture/design level.

Development (SDLC) Phase of the software development lifecycle that aims—as the name says—at actually developing the code according to design document specification (DSS).

Dining philosophers problem In concurrent programming, a problem known for explaining deadlocks and race conditions happening in a concurrent access to shared resources.

Doubly linked list A data structure where each element is represented as a node with a reference to the previous and subsequent element in the list.

Durability In concurrent programming, this property ensures that a transaction performed on the system must persist over time

Facade Structural design pattern that provides a simpler interface for different other more complex interfaces.

Factory method Creational design pattern that simplifies creating objects in such a way that there is no need to specify the specific class that needs to be created.

Fail safe Fundamental security principle. It states that if a system fails, it should fail to a state in which security and data are not compromised.

Fairness Property of concurrent systems that specify how requests are handled and served.

Feature density Design smell that happens when a component implements more than a single functionality.

Firefighting In software development, it is a condition that happens when different priorities (e.g., writing a functionality or fixing a bug) take over on each other causing a lot of context changes.

First lady components Design smell that is exhibited by a component that handles so much logic and functionalities.

FURPS+ Acronym that defines five main categories of software requirements: functional, usability, reliability, performance, and supportability. The + into the acronym indicates a set of additional requirements: implementation, interfaces, packaging, operations, and legal.

Health status In software, it indicates the overall healthiness of the system in terms of design, architecture, code, and processes.

Human resources People participating in the workforce of an organization.

Inheritance Basic property of object-oriented programming that allows a new object to take on and or extend the functionalities of an existing one.

Inline comment Single-line comment, usually used to describe very few lines of code.

Integrity Fundamental security property that ensures that a message, data, or a transaction has not been tampered.

Internet of Things (IoT) Form of distributed computation that interrelates everyday devices including, but not limited to, smartphones, sensors, and embedded devices.

Isolation In concurrent programming, this property ensures that the output of a transaction is not visible to other transactions before it successfully completes.

Iterator Behavioral design pattern that allows to navigate elements within an object, abstracting internal management.

Keywords In programming, they indicated specific terms that are part of the syntax provided by a language.

KISS Acronym of keep it simple stupid. In programming, it is a guideline that suggests to keep the code as simple as possible. The core idea is that by doing so, it would be easier after some time to work on (extend, modify, reuse) the same piece of code.

Lazy initialization Creational design pattern that allows to instantiate an object only when actually required.

Least common mechanism Fundamental security principle. It states that a minimum number of protection mechanisms should be common to users, since shared access paths may lead to information leakage.

Least privilege Security principle that requires that any subject should be given the minimum possible privilege on the minimum portion of resources for the minimum amount of time.

Linked list A data structure where each element is represented as a node with a reference to the subsequent element in the list.

Lesson learned Observation of an already executed project that should be taken into account in future projects.

Liveness Property that needs to be enforced to prove the correctness of a concurrent system. Liveness ensures that something "good" will eventually happen.

Magic numbers In programming, magic numbers are fixed values associated to variable or constant with no actual meaning.

Maintainability Property and requirement of software systems. It expresses how easy the code can be maintained (modify, extend, refactor) over time.

Mashed component Design smell that happens when a single functionality is scattered on different places on the code.

Mesh component Design smell that happens when components are heavily coupled with a lot of dependencies and oftentimes without clear and well-defined patterns.

Minimum viable product (MVP) In lean methodologies, it is defined as the minimum product that needs to be released which has the maximum return of investment (ROI).

Modifier In object-oriented programming, modifiers are keywords specific to the programming language that define how classes and methods can be accessed.

Name mangling Way to designate methods and variables as private in Python.

Non-repudiation Fundamental security principle. When enforced, any action performed cannot be denied.

Not my responsibility component Design smell that happens when a component delegates its own (logical) functionality to other components.

Observer Behavioral design pattern used when components need updates notification. According to this pattern, a component—whose state needs to be notified—stores a list of dependencies. Each and every time a change occurs, it notifies it to its stored list.

Parallel programming Refers to the ability of a software system to simultaneously execute multiple independent pieces of computation without affecting the final result.

Parameterization In programming, it refers to the usage of input variables as input to method, functions, or routines.

Pareto principle This principle—also known as the 80/20 rule—states that 20% of work causes 80% of the result.

Performances The speed at which a block of code is executed.

Post-condition A statement describing the condition which needs to hold true after the method or function has performed its duties.

Pre-condition Set of conditions that need to hold true when the method or function is called.

Problem statement Clear description of a specific issue that needs to be addressed.

Process In concurrent programming, a process is a tool that the operating systems use to run programs.

Productivity Often used as a measure of how well a team is performing.

Prototype In programming, a prototype is a codebase created in order to validate a concept. Hence, it is oftentimes not complete in functionalities: it includes just the necessary logic to prove a concept, idea, or algorithm.

Publisher-subscriber Behavioral design pattern used to monitor state changes. Similar to the observer pattern, but the dependency between who publishes and who gets the update is managed by a third-party object oftentimes referred to as broker.

Queue Basic data structure that manages elements in first in, first out (FIFO) policy.

Readability Property of software systems aiming at making the code easily understandable.

Race condition In concurrent programming, a race condition happens when the correctness of the system depends on scheduling and interleaving times of processes or threads.

Release (SDLC) Last phase in the software development lifecycle, where a product is released in the market.

Reliability Property of software system that focuses on failures and their impact.

Requirements (SDLC) Initial phase of the software development lifecycle focused on gathering information needed to be used to shape the project in terms of approach, feasibility, and operational and technical aspects.

Return of investment (ROI) A measure used to evaluate the value (e.g., efficiency, effectiveness) of an investment.

Reusability Property of software systems aimed at using methodologies and techniques to make the code easy to reuse in future development.

Risk Term used in project management to indicate an uncertain event or condition that, if it occurs, may have a positive or negative effect on one or more objectives. In the context of information security, it only refers to negative impacts and it expresses the likelihood of something bad happening.

Safety In concurrent programming, safety is the property that ensures that nothing "bad" will happen.

Secure software development lifecycle (SSDLC) Term used to refer to a software development lifecycle, where effort is done to embed security in the process.

Security General property of a system (e.g., a computer, information, and software) that embraces its protection against threats.

Security by design Refers to the need of software to be born as secure. It is designed from the ground up to be secure.

Security by obscurity In information security, it refers to recurring to hiding security mechanisms with the belief that it would increase its security. This is a very old approach and not believed to be appropriate anymore.

Security code review Code review, specifically designed to check the system against security defects.

Segregation of duties Security principle that states that no person should be given responsibility or access to more than one related function.

Singleton Creational design pattern. It restricts the number of instances of a class to a single one within the system.

SMART Acronym for specific, measurable, achievable, realistic, time bound.

Software architecture High-level view of a software.

Software development life cycle (SDLC) In simple words, it is the process of building software.

Spaghetti code Unstructured and difficult to maintain code.

Speedup Measure used to compare performances of two systems running the same program.

Starvation In concurrent programming, it happens when a piece of code never has a chance to run.

State Behavioral design pattern that enables context-aware objects.

Stack Data structure where elements are managed accordingly to a last in, first out (LIFO) policy.

Static application security testing (SAST) In security, a methodology aimed at analyzing source code in order to find security vulnerabilities.

Testing (SDLC) Phase of the software development lifecycle aimed at searching, reporting, monitoring, and fixing defects in a product or system.

Thread In concurrent and parallel programming, threads are mini-blocks of code (sub-tasks) that can run within a process.

Thread safety In concurrent programming, it is a property needed to guarantee correctness in concurrent software programs. An object is defined thread safe if, when accessed by multiple threads, its execution is correct, independently from thread's interleaving or scheduling.

Threat In security, a threat is the possible danger arising from the exploitation of a vulnerability that may result in harm to a system and an organization.

Unstable dependency Design smell that happens if a component depends on a less stable one.

User interface (UI) A graphical representation of data and services that allows for simplified interactions between a user and a computer system.

Visitor Behavioral design pattern. It allows to decouple operational logic (i.e., algorithms) that would be otherwise scattered throughout different similar objects.

Vulnerability In security, a vulnerability is the channel that can be exploited to make a risk real.

Waterfall Methodology used in project management and software engineering. If used, all the phases of the software development lifecycle are executed in isolation and sequentially.

Weakest link Security principle that states the importance of identification and mitigation of the weakest mechanisms in the security chain.

References

British Standard Institute, I. t. (2004). Security techniques, Management of information and communications technology security, Part 1: Concepts and models for information and communications technology security management BS ISO/IEC 13335-1-2004.

Cohen Jason. Best Kept Secrets of Peer Code Review. Smart Bear, 2006.

Cormen, Thomas H., et al. *Introduction to Algorithms*. MIT Press, 2009.

D'Ambros, M., Bacchelli, A., & Lanza, M. (2010, July). *On the impact of design flaws on software defects*. In Quality Software (QSIC), 2010 10th International Conference on (pp. 23–31). IEEE.

Dijkstra, E. W. "Go to statement considered harmful." In *Software Pioneers* (pp. 351–355). Springer, 2002.

Fontana, Francesca Arcelli, et al. "Arcan: A tool for architectural smells detection." 2017 IEEE International Conf. on Software Architecture Workshops, ICSA Workshops 2017, Gothenburg, Sweden, April 5–7. 2017.

Fowler, Martin. *Patterns of enterprise application architecture*. Addison-Wesley Longman Publishing Co., 2002.

Fowler, Martin. *Code Smell*, https://martinfowler.com/bliki/CodeSmell.html, 2006. Last accessed June 2020.

Fowler, Martin, et al. *Refactoring: improving the design of existing code*. Addison-Wesley Professional, 1999.

Galvis, Al. *Messaging Design Pattern and Pattern Implementation*. 17th conference on Pattern Languages of Programs-PLoP. 2010.

Gamma, Erich, et al. *Design patterns: elements of reusable object-oriented software*. Addison-Wesley Professional, 1994.

Ganesh, S. G., Tushar Sharma, and Girish Suryanarayana. *Towards a Principle-based Classification of Structural Design Smells*. Journal of Object Technology, 12(2), 1–1, 2013.

GitLab. Static Application Security Testing (SAST), `https://docs.gitlab.com/ee/user/application_security/sast/`.Llast accessed June 2020.

Glib, Tom, Graham Dorothy. *Software Inspection*. Addison-Wesley Professional, 1994.

Grady, Robert B. *Practical Software Metrics for Project Management and Process Improvement*. Prentice Hall, 1992.

Herlihy, Maurice, and Nir Shavit. *The art of multiprocessor programming*. Morgan Kaufmann, 2011.

Hernandez, Steven. *Official (ISC)2 Guide to the CISSP CBK*. Auerbach Publications, 2012.

Hill, Mark D., and Michael R. Marty. *Amdahl's law in the multicore era*. Computer 41.7, 2008.

Ipek Ozkaya. Strategic Management of Architectural Technical Debt. SEI Agile Blog. `https://insights.sei.cmu.edu/sei_blog/2012/07/strategic-management-of-architectural-technical-debt.html`. 2016. Last accessed on June 2020.

Li, Wei and Raed Shatnawi, "An Empirical Study of the Bad Smells and Class Error Probability in the Post-Release Object-Oriented System Evolution," *Journal of Systems and Software*, 80(7): pp. 1120–1128, 2007.

Martin, Robert C. Clean Code: A Handbook of Agile Software Craftsmanship. Pearson Education, 2009.

Micha Gorelick and Ian Ozsvald. *High Performance Python: Practical Performant Programming for Humans*, 2nd ed. O' Reilly Media, 2020.

National Vulnerability Database – statistics, `https://nvd.nist.gov/vuln/search/statistics?form_type=Basic&results_type=statistics&search_type=all`. Last accessed June 2020.

OWASP Developer Guide. `https://github.com/OWASP/DevGuide`. Last accessed on May 2018.

OWASP Source Code Analysis Tools. `https://owasp.org/www-community/Source_Code_Analysis_Tools`. Last accessed June 2020.

Python Software Foundation Style Guide for Python Code. `https://www.python.org/dev/peps/pep-0008/`, 2016. Last accessed June 2020.

Python Software Foundation. Concurrent Execution, `https://docs.python.org/3/library/concurrency.html`. Last accessed June 2020.

Randell, Brian. Software engineering in 1968. In *Proceedings of the 4th international conference on Software engineering* (pp. 1–10). IEEE Press. September 1979.

Sharma, Tushar. Designite-tools, `www.designite-tools.com/blog/does-your-architecture-smell`. 2017. Last accessed on June 2020.

Sharma, Tushar. "Does Your Architecture Smell? Design Smells. Managing Technical Debt," `www.designsmells.com/articles/does-your-architecture-smell/`. Last accessed on June 2020.

Sphinx. `www.sphinx-doc.org/en/master/`. Last accessed June 2020.

Suryanarayana, Girish, Ganesh Samarthyam, and Tushar Sharma. *Refactoring for software design smells: managing technical debt*. Morgan Kaufmann, 2014.

Weigers, Karl. *Peer Reviews in Software*. Addison-Wesley Professional, 2002.

Yurisich, Andrew. How to Write Unmaintainable Code. `https://github.com/Droogans/unmaintainable-code`. Last accessed on June 2020.

Zen of Python. `www.python.org/dev/peps/pep-0020/`. Last accessed on June 2020.

Index

Printed in the United States
By Bookmasters